57 games

TO PLAY IN THE LIBRARY OR CLASSROOM

Carol K. Lee
and
Fay Edwards

Alleyside Press

Fort Atkinson, Wisconsin

Published by Alleyside Press, an imprint of Highsmith Press LLC
Highsmith Press
W5527 Highway 106
P.O. Box 800
Fort Atkinson, Wisconsin 53538-0800

1-800-558-2110

Cover design: Cyrus Highsmith

The paper used in this publication meets the minimum requirements of American National Standard for Information Science — Permanence of Paper for Printed Library Material. ANSI/NISO Z39.48-1992.

Library of Congress Cataloging-in-Publication Data
   Lee, Carol K.
      57 games to play in the library or classroom / Carol K. Lee and
   Fay Edwards.
         p. cm.
      Rev. ed. of: 50 games to play in the library or classroom.
      Includes index.
      ISBN 1-57950-014-5 (paper : alk. paper)
      1. Library orientation for school children. 2. Elementary school
   libraries--Problems, exercises, etc. 3. Educational games.
   I. Edwards, Fay. II. Lee, Carol K. 50 games to play in the library
   or classroom. III. Title.
   Z711.2.L45 1997
   027.62 ' 5--dc21   97-27786
                                                                           CIP

Contents

Introduction

SINCE THE PUBLICATION of *50 Games to Play in the Library or Classroom*, the eighteen years of using games in teaching have extended to twenty-eight years. The games continue to be effective tools to promote reading interest and to reinforce research skills taught in both the classroom and the media center. Students still love to play the games.

Changes have resulted from the advances in instructional technology and its use in the curriculum. Access to information resources through CD-ROMs and the Internet, interactive programs, and the automation of the media center have revolutionized the media program.

This game book has been thoroughly revised to exclude references to materials and equipment considered obsolete. Several games have been deleted from the original book and eleven more have been added. Instead of 50 games, there are 57 games.

The response to the first book during its nine years of publication has been overwhelming. Continued sales of the book indicate that teachers and media specialists adapted the games to meet the changes brought on by new technologies.

We hope that this revised edition will make it easier to use and provide you with a larger resource of game ideas.

As stated in the introduction to the first book:

Most of our games are board games rather than worksheets or interest-center activities. They are designed for use with the entire class, but they also can be used with smaller groups.

We have provided sample questions to use with the games and have suggested alternative ways to use certain games. We have provided patterns.

Try a game or two. You will be pleased to see how effectively students learn with this a fun approach.

Helpful Hints

1. Most games can be set up in several different formats—mat boards, posterboards, pizza wheels, flannelboard, or even temporarily on a chalkboard or overhead projector.

2. Ask yourself when you begin: "How can I alter this game to fit the materials I have and the skills I wish to develop?" Tailor the sample questions to the abilities of your own students.

3. Although dimensions for the game materials are often suggested in this handbook, they are only loose guidelines. You can easily change the sizes and even shapes of the games to suit your available materials.

4. Paste pockets (library or stationery) on the backs of your games to store the game cards.

5. You can use the backs of commercial game boards for your own games or activities. When preparing laminated sheets, plan to double-face those, too.

6. By merely altering the rules a little or developing several sets of questions, many games can be used with several different grade levels.

7. As you progress with making a game, step back from it the distance your students will normally be seated to check on its visibility by the class.

8. Be alert to the many attractive materials you can use—wallpaper, wrapping paper, greeting cards. Publishers' catalogs are a great source for pictures, as are Scholastic and Troll paperback forms.

9. A game board can be hinged not only once but twice, which allows it to stand freely if it has been made on a mat board. (Ask picture framing businesses for discards). Hinging also allows you to use two boards that were too small otherwise, and provides easier storage.

10. Save game parts such as tokens, dice, and spinners from discarded commercial games.

11. For game boards that require numbers, use pattern pages 128–129, or cut up old calendar sheets.

12. A bank of sample questions for board games begins on page 131. You'll probably want to develop your own "question bank" as time goes on—3x5" index cards are a handy way to organize them.

13. For games that call for book pockets, you can also use regular envelopes, but cut them off at the ends.

14. If clothespins cannot be found, you might use colored hair clips, or clamps found in a hardware store. Office supply catalogs or stores may also have large colored clips that will work as game pieces.

Glad Book, Sad Book

Purpose

To discuss care of books and/or manners used in the media center.

To Make

Cut the desired number of "face" circles—about fourteen. Paste along the edges of the posterboard. Draw mostly happy faces. Attach a book pocket to hold GO cards (six). GO cards are awarded each time a team passes the start arrow.

Make a "face" cube or spinner to determine game moves.

Create game pieces by coloring the tops of clothespins or by using colored paper or hair clips.

To Play

Divide the class into two teams. Team members alternately use the cube or spinner to determine a glad or sad face square and move their team game piece. To remain on that face, the player offers a statement of either desirable or undesirable manners concerning books, the library, or the use of computers— desirable manners for a glad face and undesirable manners for a sad one.

When a team passes the start arrow, it may either be declared winner or earn a GO card and play continues. The winning team is the one with the most GO cards at the end of the time limit.

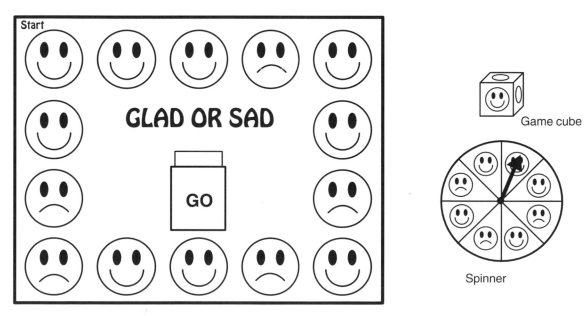

Game board

Game cube

Spinner

Media Manners

Purpose

To discuss/review good manners used in the media center.

To Make

Reproduce the game as shown below on posterboard. Paste down two library pockets—one a happy face, one sad.

Print or type about twenty cards that will fit in the pockets (2x4") which state manners you wish to reinforce—write twice as many positive as negative ones. (*See the following page for samples.*) Also state on each card the number of moves the player may make forward (if happy) or backward (if sad).

To Play

Divide the class into two teams. Opposing players alternately select a card from the Media Manners stack, which is face down on the game board or table.

Each player must read the statement on their card aloud and then file the card in the correct pocket. If correct, they move as directed by the card on the board, using clothespins, large clips or other game pieces. The team completing the moves around the board first is the winner. You will probably want to encourage discussion on the manners as the game proceeds.

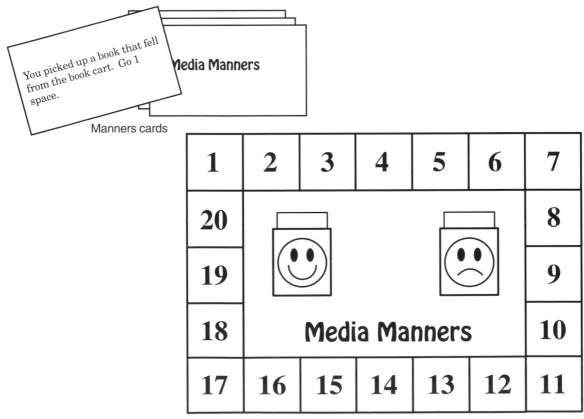

You picked up a book that fell from the book cart. Go 1 space.

Media Manners

Manners cards

1	2	3	4	5	6	7
20						8
19						9
18		Media Manners				10
17	16	15	14	13	12	11

Game board

Media Manners Sample Cards

(Use twice as many positive cards as negative ones.)

Sample Happy Cards

You are a good listener in the media center. Go 2 spaces.

You walked quietly in the media center. Go 3 spaces.

When you left the table, you pushed in your chair. Go 1 space.

You returned your book on time. Go 3 spaces.

You used a bookmark to keep your place in your book. Go 1 space.

You put the pencil back in the pencil can. Go 1 space.

You showed the media specialist a tear in a library book. Go 1 space.

You reminded your friend not to twirl his book on the table. Go 1 space.

You found a book upside down on the shelf and turned it around. Go 1 space.

You showed a new student how we use the media center computer. Go 1 space.

You lined up nicely when it was time to go. Go 2 spaces.

You raised your hand when you wanted to share an idea with the class. Go 2 spaces.

You followed the rules for sharing time on the computer. Go 2 spaces.

When you came to the media center with your class, you seated yourself immediately. Go 1 space.

You picked up a book that fell from the book cart. Go 1 space.

You returned the magazine you were browsing to the correct stack. Go 1 space.

You waited patiently in the check-out line. Go 3 spaces.

You helped another student find information in the electronic encyclopedia. Go 2 spaces.

Sample Sad Cards

You used a pencil for a bookmark. Go back 1 space.

You left your book on the playground. Go back 2 spaces.

Your little brother tore the date due out of your book. Go back 2 spaces.

You did not protect your library book from the rain. Go back 2 spaces.

Your dog chewed your library book. Go back 3 spaces.

You got chocolate fingerprints on some pages. Go back 3 spaces.

You left your shelf marker on the table. Go back 1 space.

You forgot to close the card catalog drawers. Go back 1 space.

You noisily interrupted another class when you came to return your book. Go back 2 spaces.

Your hands were sticky when you used the computer. Go back 1 space.

Media Center Alphabet

Purpose

To review terminology, manners, and the care of materials used in the media center.

To Make

Mount large letters of the alphabet (4x5") on the fronts of large cards (7x8"). On the back of each card, print the verse that accompanies each letter so it can be read aloud to the class as you go through the alphabet. Discuss as needed.

A... is the **Alphabet** we all will now do and talk of the media center before we are through.

B... is the **Biography**—famous people we know. Reading about them helps us to grow.

C... is for **Computer Catalog** which helps us to find the type of book we have on our mind.

D... is the **Date** your book should return. To bring it on time is important to learn.

E... is **Erasers**. Please use on a spot where marks appear, whether you made them or not.

F... is **Fiction**. We know it's not true. Be sure to read some nonfiction, too.

G... is **Great**, the way books will stay, if we bring clean hands on library day.

H... is **How** to care for our books. They're more fun to use the nicer they look.

I... I love the media center. I hope you do, too. Let's see what fun things we all can do.

J... is **Join** in courtesy rules so things will be pleasant all 'round the school.

K... **Keep** books at home in a place you know, so you can find them when it's time to go.

L... is **Library**. We call ours the media center.

M... a reminder to **Mark** your place. Then you won't have to lay the book on its face.

N... is **Now**. Let's really get with it, so the media center will be a fun place to visit.

O... is **Open** the book to see, if it's really what you want it to be.

P... is the **Page** we must turn with care, or soon it might just develop a tear.

Q... is the **Quiet** manners we show, from the time we come in till the time we go.

R.. is **Rain,** which will ruin your book. Please protect the one you took.

S... is **Sticky**—cookies, candy, and gum. A book that is messy is really not fun.

T... is **Title**—the name of a book. We have lots of titles. Just take a look.

U... is **Up** where your books should go, so puppies and babies won't tear them, you know.

V... is "Oh, so **Very** good." That's what we'll say, when you do as you should.

W... is the **Writing** in a good fiction book. Sometimes its funny or sad or just so exciting.

X... marks the spot where I laid my book down. Oh, how I wish it hadn't been on the ground!

Y... is for **You** as well as for me. Let's all keep the media center as it should be.

Z.. is the letter that ends our say. We hope you remember what we've said today.

Keep the Media Center Alphabet in your mind and

We'll have a great year, I'm sure you'll find.

Pitch Points

Purpose

A general game to be used with any skill. Type and difficulty of the questions will determine grade level.

To Make

Use masking tape to tape 5"-square plastic grocery cartons (the kind used to package mushrooms) in clusters of four as shown below. You may use two clusters of four (eight cartons) or four clusters of four (sixteen cartons).

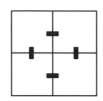

Tape cartons in clusters

Arrange the clusters to fit your playing area and tape them together.

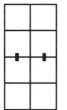 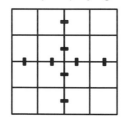 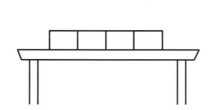

Two clusters   Four clusters   Place the completed game board on
a table or other flat surface.

Duplicate the number squares from the following page. Cut the squares out and place them in the bottoms of the cartons.

To Play

You will need two large buttons to pitch. Place cartons in a central location, resting flat on the table. Use masking tape to designate a line from which students will pitch the buttons.

Divide the class into two teams. Ask the first player a question. If the answer is correct, the student pitches the team button into a carton. The team receives the points indicated on the card in the bottom of the carton.

Ask the next question of the other team, and continue by alternating questions whether student offers correct answer or not. The team with the most points wins the game.

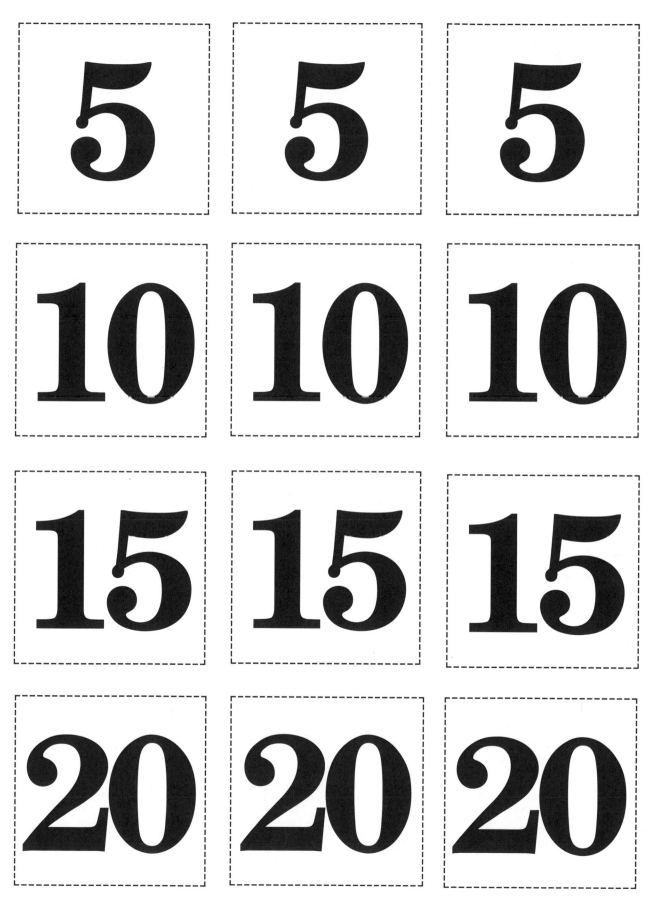

Tic Tac Toe

Purpose

A general board game to review any skill. Difficulty of questions will determine grade level.

To Make

Cut out circles in the center of nine book pockets. Then paste the pockets in a tic-tac-toe position as shown. Or tape nine slots on a posterboard.

Make cards with Xs and Os to be placed during the game.

To Play

Divide the group into two teams. Assign the X to one team and the O to the other. Ask the first player a question. If the answer is correct, have the player put his team's mark on the board. If incorrect, no mark is placed. Continue the game by asking the next question of the other team. Alternate turns until one team gets Tic-Tac-Toe or three of the same marks in a row.

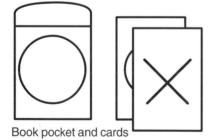

Book pocket and cards

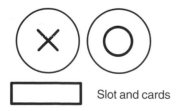

Slot and cards

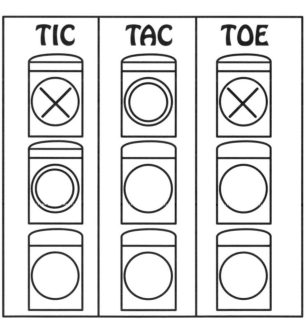

Game board

Library Speedway

Purpose

A general board game to be used with all skills.

To Make

You need three lengths of board 10x26". Cut six lengths of posterboard 1x26" to form a double tray across the boards for the "racetrack." Paste only the bottom edges of the trays down on the boards so the two race cars can move through the slot formed by the tray. Decorate the game board with the checkerboard flags.

Cut out two cars (from the pattern) using heavy paper and decorate.

Label the board as shown, then hinge.

A spinner or cube is needed to indicate game moves.

To Play

Divide the class into two teams. As members of each team alternately answer skill questions correctly, they spin the spinner (or roll the cube) and move the team car accordingly. If the car lands on PASS, move ahead one space; if on PIT STOP, lose one turn.

An incorrect answer forfeits the team's turn. The winning team is the first to complete the race.

Library Speedway

Start				Pass	Pit Stop				Finish

Game board

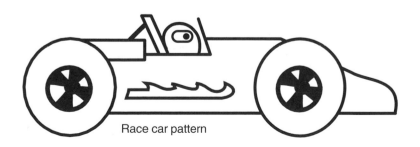

Race car pattern

Ups and Downs

Purpose

A general board game to be used with any skill. The type and difficulty of the questions determines grade level.

To Make

Use a posterboard and the example below to make the game board. Cut the "up" arrows from green construction paper and the "down" arrows from red construction paper. Do not have too many "down" or go back arrows. Paste the arrows on the numbered board in any way you desire.

You will need two small note stickers to use as markers and a dice or spinner. Label the note stickers Team 1 and Team 2, or give the teams names.

To Play

Divide the class into two teams. Ask the first player a question. If the response is correct, the player rolls the dice or spins the spinner. Move the appropriate sticker the number of jumps indicated. If the marker lands on an "up" arrow, move ahead to the point of the arrow. If the marker lands on a "down" arrow, move back to the point of the arrow.

Alternate asking the teams questions. The first to reach the last number is the winner.

Ups and Downs					
36	35	34	33	32	31
25	26	27	28	29	30
24	23	22	21	20	19
13	14	15	16	17	18
12	11	10	9	8	7
1 Start	2	3	4	5	6

Game board

Star Walk

Purpose

A general board game to be used with any set of skill questions. In this example, it is a biography study. *(See sample questions on page 19)*

To Make

Cut six each of red, white and blue stars from the star pattern. Paste around a posterboard, alternating colors. Decorate with a title and the "astronaut" pattern on the next page if you wish.

Make a spinner or cube in red, white, and blue.

Use clothespins, clamps or large clips for team moves.

To Play

Divide the class into two teams. Clip the clothespins on START. Opposing players alternately answer questions. If correct, move to the next star of the color indicated by the spinner.

The first team to completely circle the board wins.

Game board

Star Walk

Star pattern

Astronaut pattern

Star Walk Questions

1. What is a biography? *(Book about a real person)*

2. What is an autobiography? *(Book about a person, written by that person him- or herself)*

3. How do you know when you have a biography book? *(B on spine)*

4. How are the biography books arranged on the shelf?
   (Alphabetically by the last name of person the book is about)

5. Where do the letters on the second line of the call number come from?
   (First three letters of the last name of person book is about)

6. If a biography were written about you, what would the call number be?
   (Have several students come to the chalkboard, in turn, and write their call number. Use each as a game move.)

7. First, middle or last—in which area of the biography section would books about these people be found?

Abraham Lincoln	Thomas Alva Edison
Rachel Carson	Harriet Tubman
Martin Luther King, Jr.	Eleanor Roosevelt

8. Would a book about Paul Bunyan be a biography? *(No, a tall tale)*

*9. Name a famous person that a biography might be written about.

*10. What would be the call number of the person just named.

11. Are biographies written only about people who have died. *(No)*

12. What is a collective biography? *(One book containing the life stories of several people)*

13. What would be the call number for a person known basically by one name only?
    (Use the first three letters of first name.

14. For example, Queen Elizabeth. *(B/ELI)*

15. For example, Pocahontas. *(B/Poc)*

16. Name one type of information a computer catalog gives on a biography?
    (1)Whether available. 2) How many copies available. 3) Titles, authors)

If feasible in your library, have a student go to the biography shelf to locate a specific book. This could be asked several times.

*Use these two questions alternately several times. Award a game move for each correct answer.

Batter Up

Purpose

A general game format to be used with any set of skill questions you want to review. Although suggested for intermediate grades, even first graders understand baseball.

To Make

Use at least a 13"-square board or draw a square to the edges of a pizza wheel or posterboard circle. You can also draw the game on a chalkboard.

Use spring clothespins, large clips or clamps to move around the bases. Decorate them as "players" if you wish.

Brighten the "infield" with a baseball motif or use the pattern of a player on the following page.

To Play

Divide the class into two teams. Each student will take a turn "at bat" by trying to answer a library skill question.

With each correct answer, a clothespin "player" moves to a base. After three bases are "loaded," the next correct answer brings in the run.

After three outs, the opposing team comes to bat. The team with the most runs wins.

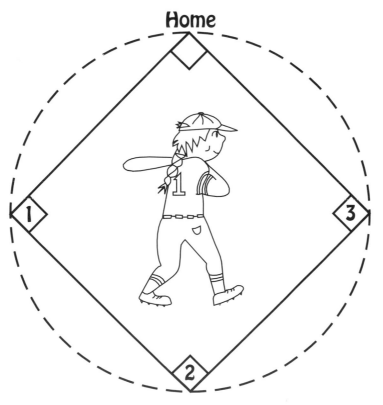

Game board

Optional pattern for Batter Up game board

Spin-A-Round

Purpose

To review skills in four major areas. Difficulty is determined by questions.

To Make

Draw a large circle on a posterboard. Divide this circle into four parts. You can make the four segments out of four colors of construction paper. Write these words in the segments.

Manners	Technology (or Media)
Call Numbers	Easy Fiction (or fiction)

Put a spinner in the center of the circle. Paste four book pockets in the four corners of the board.

Cut about twelve 3x5" index cards in half (lengthwise). Write questions on these cards *(See sample questions on next page)*. Put these cards in the pockets.

To Play

Divide the class into two teams. Direct the first player to spin the spinner and draw a card from the corresponding pocket. Read the question and give a point to that team if the answer is correct.

Follow the same procedure with a player from the other team and continue alternating teams until the game time is up. The team with the most points wins the game.

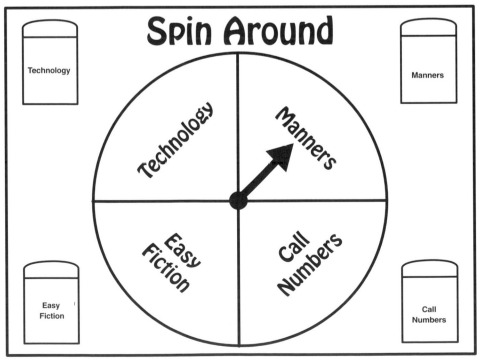

Game board

Spin-A-Round Sample Questions

Manners

1. What must you always bring to the library? *(Pencil)*

2. What must you use when you to to the shelf? *(Shelf marker)*

3. What must you use to mark a place in a book? *(Bookmark)*

4. Finish the sentence: You should always protect a book from _____.
   (The rain, your baby sister, pets)

5. You should put a book back on the shelf so the _____ can be seen. *(Title)*

6. Never _____ a book. *(Write or color in; cut)*

7. Who mends the tears in a book? *(Librarian of library assistant)*

8. Tell a rule to follow in the media center.

9. Only write your name on a _____ . *(Book card)*

Technology / Media

Paste pictures of technology resources or media center equipment and ask students to identify the item or describe how it would be used.

Easy Fiction

1. Where is the Easy Fiction in the library?

2. What symbol is on the spine of an Easy Fiction? *(E)*

3. Do the three letters under the E stand for the title or the author's name? *(Author's name)*

4. In what order are Easy Fiction books shelved? *(Alphabetically)*

5. On the title page is this information:

   Make Way for Ducklings by Robert McCloskey

   Who is the author? What is the title?

6. Give an example of an Easy Fiction title.

7. How are Easy Fiction books different from Fiction books?
   (Easy Fiction books have more pictures; fewer words)

8. Which book would come first on the shelf? *Mop Top* by Don Freeman or *The Animal* by Lorna Balian. *(The Animal)*

Call Numbers

On each card write: Easy Fiction or Nonfiction? Then put Easy Fiction or Nonfiction call numbers on these cards. Add biography and nonbook call numbers for upper grades.

Bowling

Purpose

A general board game to review any skill. Difficulty is determined by questions.

To Make

Tape five slots on a posterboard as shown below.

Trace and cut from tagboard ten bowling pins. Number the pins. Cut ten bowling balls from construction paper. Write the questions on one side of each ball. *(See sample questions on p. 25.)*

Place the pins and balls on the gameboard as shown below.

To Play

Divide the class into two teams. Direct the starting player from one team to select a bowling ball and to proceed to name ten items that correspond to the question. As the player correctly responds, remove a pin. If that player gives ten correct responses in sequence, that team gets a strike and scores 20 points. If the player gives a wrong answer, stop and have another player from that team continue from that point. If the second player reaches ten, that team gets 15 instead of 20 points for a "spare." If the second player gives a wrong answer, then the round ends for that team with a score for just the number of pins knocked down.

Place the pins back on the board and go to the other team. The team with the most points wins the game.

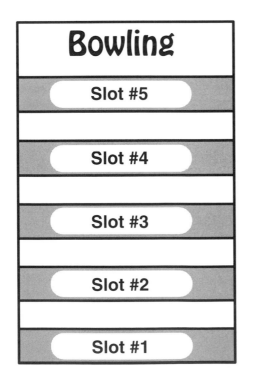

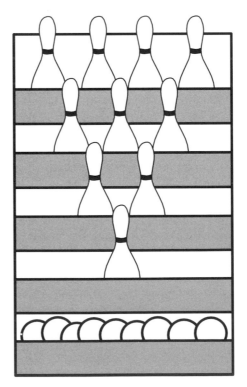

Game board

Sample Bowling Questions

Name:

1. 10 fiction titles.

2. 10 nonfiction titles.

3. 10 subjects in the 500 section.

4. 10 folk or fairy tales.

5. 10 magazines or periodicals.

6. 10 rules for proper use of the library or library books.

7. 10 biographies.

8. 10 Caldecott or Newbery Award winners.

9. 10 subjects in the 900 section.

10. 10 animal stories.

11. 10 pieces of audiovisual equipment or audiovisual materials in the media center.

12. 10 web sites.

13. 10 terms relating to the computer equipment in the media center.

14. 10 key words about _____ (a subject the class has discussed recently).

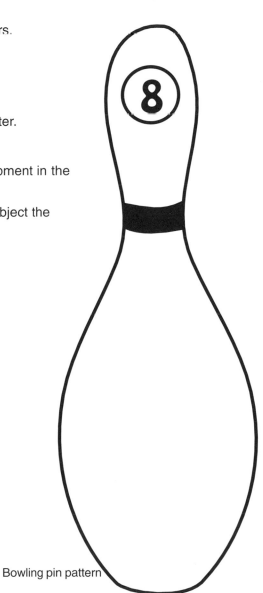

Bowling pin pattern

Grades 3–6

Risk It!

Purpose

A general board game to review any skill.

To Make

Cut 25 flaps out of five different colors of construction paper (five of each color). Tape the flaps to a posterboard five across and five down. Use the five colors to create five columns, i.e., a red column, blue column, etc. Number these flaps as shown in the sample board.

Underneath the flaps paste 1" pockets cut from book pockets or envelopes. Cut cards to insert in these pockets. Create questions in degrees of difficulty.

Make one card with the words RISK IT!

Write five topic headings on cards to be attached at the top of the board. For example: Call number; Parts of a Book; Biography; Computer Catalog; Reference.

To Play

Place question cards in the pockets with the easier questions under the five and ten point flaps.

Divide the class into two teams. Direct the first player to select a flap and read the question underneath. Have that player answer the question.

If correct, give that team the number of points on the flap. Paperclip the flap to remind the class that that question has been correctly answered.

If incorrect, do not give the correct answer. Someone may try for that question later.

If the RISK IT! card appears, direct the player to decide how many points his team wants to risk to answer that question. If the team is unable to answer correctly, the points are deducted from the points already earned.

Alternate turns and count up the score at the end of the class period. The team with the most points wins.

RISK IT!

5	5	5	5	5
10	10	10	10	10
15	15	15	15	15
20	20	20	20	20
25	25	25	25	25

Game board

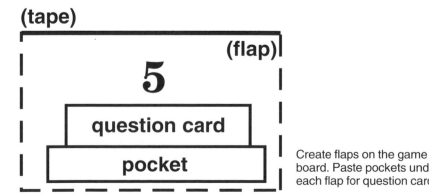

(tape)

(flap)

5

question card

pocket

Create flaps on the game board. Paste pockets under each flap for question cards.

Risk It!

You will need three copies of this page to make the Risk It! game. Cut out the rectangles on the lines.

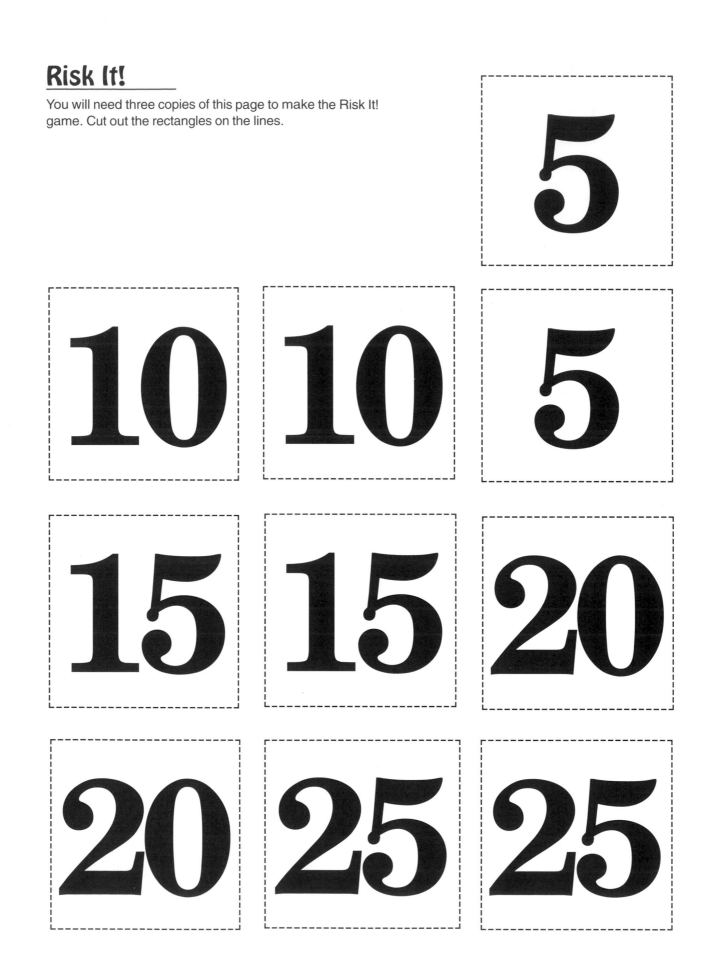

Slam! Dunk!

Purpose

A general board game to be used with any skill.

To Make

Cut three boards, 14x18". Reproduce, color, and cut out the patterns for basketballs and nets *(Patterns next page)*.

You will need 20 large "orangish" basketballs and one small one. Paste the goal patterns on two library pockets. Position and paste the goal, small ball and player patterns on two of the boards as shown on the next page. Title the third board. Cut two sturdy 1½ x14" strips. Paste along three edges only and position on the board to create slots in which to slip the balls.

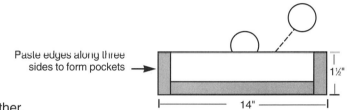

Paste edges along three sides to form pockets →

1½"

|— 14" —|

Hinge the boards together.

On the back of the large balls, print the following game directions:

On three balls: 3-POINT BASKET

On eleven balls: 2-POINT BASKET

On two balls: FOUL. OTHER TEAM EARNS 1 FREE THROW

On two balls: TURNOVER, LOSE TURN

On the front of the last two balls, print: FREE THROW. 1 POINT. Place these two balls in sight, in the trays, to be used as a counter-move when a "foul" ball is uncovered.

You can select questions in three ways:

Read from a prepared list.

Print on cards which the players will select.

Print on the basketballs.

To Play

Divide the class into two teams. Players alternately select a basketball and proceed according to directions. The "point" balls are tallied and put into the "goal" pockets as questions are answered correctly.

When a "foul" ball turns up, the opposing team puts a FREE THROW ball into their goal as a 1 point bonus, no question necessary. Questioning is then returned to the team that fouled. The team with the highest score wins.

Slam! Dunk!

Game board

Goal Pockets. Place a baskball in the "goal" for each correctly answered question.

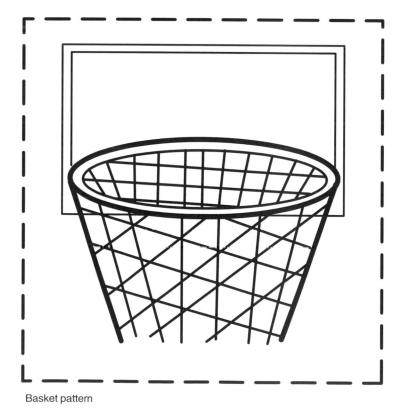

Basket pattern

Use this pattern for the small basketball for the game board, and enlarge and duplicate it for the 20 large game balls.

Slam! Dunk! Basketball players

Touchdown

Purpose

A general game format to be used with any set of skill questions you want to review.

To Make

The playing field can be drawn on any rectangular board (or chalkboard for temporary use). Approximate size of the board: 18x36" or about twice as long as it is wide. Cover the board with green paper to create the playing field.

Mark the game play with two clothespins or clips of a different color.

To Play

Let the two teams select names if you like (Rams, Packers). Place the "ball" (clothespin or clips) on the 20 yard line, where it is always "received." As long as Team A answers correctly, the ball moves down the field ten yards per question. If a goal is made, a touchdown of six points is scored. A one-point "kick" is then scored if a relatively easy question can be answered—a story-related one, for instance. Team B then "receives" on the opposite 20 yard line and tries for a touchdown.

When a question is missed, a "fumble" is declared and the opposing team takes over on that yardage. This reverses play to the opposite goal. The team with the most touchdowns wins.

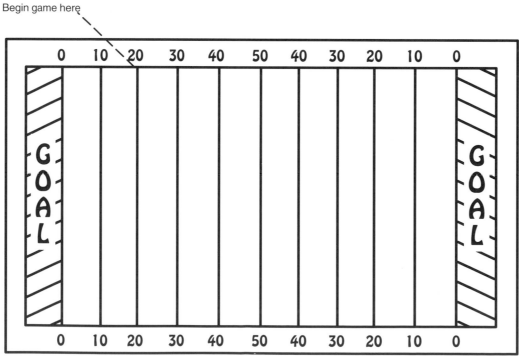

Game board

Quiz Game with Lap Chalkboards

Purpose

A general game to be used with any skill. Difficulty of questions determines grade level.

To Play

You will need about six lap chalkboards (sometimes called chalkboard slates).

Divide the class into groups of four to five students.

Decide on each team's recorder or have each team select a recorder. Hand out chalkboards, erasers, and chalk (one of each to each team.)

Ask a question. The teams decide on the answer by group consensus. The recorder writes the answer.

Direct the recorders to hold up the answers at the command, "Boards Up!" Give each team that has the correct answer a point. Then direct them with a "Boards Down, Erase!" command. The recorder is the only one to write and erase the team's answers.

Continue until all questions have been asked. Add up the scores and announce the results.

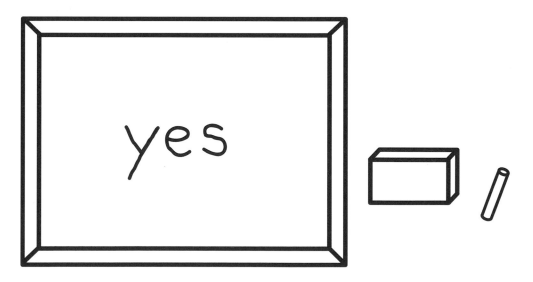

Reminder: Give multiple choice questions or questions that require minimum writing as the space on the board is limited.

Bingo Games

Purpose

A game format to review any skill. Difficulty of questions determines grade level. *(Sample questions are provided at the back of this book.)*

To Make

Create playing boards. If you are making boards with nine squares, try creating a master list of at least twenty items if you can. Using pictures for the items whenever possible also works well. You can use the backs of the boards for a different Bingo game or reproduce a title page or Dewey Decimal chart.

Make a master board for each set and a master set of cards. Duplicate and paste up enough cards so that each student has a unique Bingo card. Use for skills discussion if you choose.

Use pennies, buttons , seeds or any other small item for markers.

To Play

Randomly call out terms on the Bingo boards until a student has BINGO. Use the master board to keep track of items that have been called out.

Sample Cards

Title Page	©	Computer Catalog
Biography	Reference	Globe
Fiction	Index	Fairy Tales

Skills Bingo

Corduroy	Clifford	Miss Nelson
Amelia Bedelia	Ping	Arthur
Cat in the Hat	Curious George	Harold and his Crayon

Story Bingo

Skills Bingo
Master Board

Author	☐	Illustrator	☐
Biography	☐	Index	☐
Call number	☐	Magazine	☐
Computer Catalog	☐	Nonfiction	☐
Contents	☐	Publisher	☐
Copyright	☐	Reference	☐
Fairy tales	☐	Spine	☐
Fiction	☐	Story Coll.	☐
Globe	☐	Subject	☐
Glossary	☐	Title page	☐

Other possible Bingo games

Audiovisual	Authors	Caldecott
Call Numbers	Holidays	Newbery
Nonfiction	Stories or folktales	Technology

Seasonal Wheels/ Boards

Purpose

To review any skill or storybook by using a seasonal theme. Difficulty of questions determines grade level.

To Make

On any shape board, draw off blocks around the outer edge. Numbering the blocks is optional. Decorate with seasonal pictures. Title the game or let the pictures denote the theme. Use a spinner or dice to determine game moves.

Optional method: In lieu of cut pictures and a spinner or dice, use duplicate sets of holiday stickers. Paste one set of stickers randomly in the blocks around the board. Paste the second set of stickers on small cards (3x3").

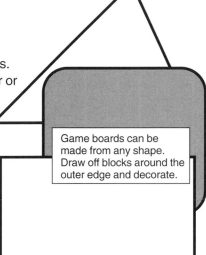

Game boards can be made from any shape. Draw off blocks around the outer edge and decorate.

To Play

Divide the class into two teams. Use a spinner or cube to determine game moves. Direct questions alternately to team players, correct answers are required to move forward. If the game board is used in an upright position, team moves can be made with large clips. If the game is used on a flat surface, team moves can be made with markers such as buttons or seeds.

Optional method: Stack the cards face down in the center of the game board, or at the side of a stand-up board. To determine game moves, the player turns over the top card and moves to the block that matches the sticker card when a question has been correctly answered. To fatten the deck, have several extra cards with only numbers that tell the player how many moves to make.

Game board

Spelling Down the Media Center

Purpose

To reinforce the spelling of basic library language and foster recognition of the words.

To Play

Allow for two consecutive class periods. On the first day, the class volunteers a list of at least twenty library-related words, which are recorded on the chalkboard. Conduct whatever discussion is needed to draw out the list.

Suggested words:

spine	subject	nonfiction	dictionary
index	media center	call number	title page
fiction	contents	reference	copyright
title	biography	illustrator	computer
author	glossary	publisher	foreword
OPAC	keyword	desktop	terminal
e-mail	encyclopedia	bibliography	magazine
software	Internet	shut down	

Each student copies the list to study as "homework."

If you prefer to eliminate Day 1 (and its review possibilities), distribute a spelling list you have already prepared in advance of the "spell-down."

The game is played on the second day. Conduct like any spelling bee. A student who misspells is seated. Continue through the list until only one student is standing. Award a small prize if you wish.

Media Hunt

Purpose

To review audiovisual terms.

To Make

On the outer edge of a posterboard, draw animal tracks or print tracks made from a potato. Cut and paste at random, between the tracks, pictures of audiovisual equipment.

Write the title MEDIA HUNT in the center of the board.

Prepare a set of 25 question cards with a designated number of jumps for the correct answer.

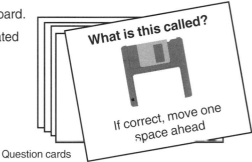

Question cards

To Play

Divide the class into two teams. Direct the first player of Team A to draw a question card and answer that question. If correct, move with a large clip or clamp the number of times indicated. If not, leave the marker and switch to Team B, following the same procedure. If a team lands on a picture, have that player identify the equipment for a 1 jump bonus.

The first team to circle the board wins the game.

Game board

Media Hunt Questions

1. What is another word for library?

    a. media center
    b. laboratory
    c. aquarium
    (a. media center)

2. The screen is on the

    a. disk drive
    b. monitor
    c. keyboard
    (b. monitor)

3. What part of the computer is this? *(Picture of keyboard)*

4. A globe shows you

    a. both land and water areas
    b. ponds and streams
    c. counties and small towns
    (a. both land and water areas)

5. True or False? The computer catalog lists audiovisual materials that are in the library?
    (True)

6. What is this called? *(picture of a CD-ROM, laser disk, computer diskette, etc.)*

7. True or False? A globe shows you the roads and highways of a country? *(False)*

8. What is another name for a librarian?

    a. custodian
    b. publisher
    c. media specialist
    (c. media specialist)

9. A CD is an example of

    a. printed material
    b. an audiovisual material
    c. a magazine or a periodical
    (b. an audiovisual material)

10. Where should you handle or hold a disk?   *(By the label)*

11. Which of these is not a nonbook material?

    a. audiocassette   b. periodical   c. CD-ROM   *(b. periodical)*

12. What is the call number for a video recording? *(VR, depends on the media center)*

13. What is the screen of a computer called? *(Desktop)*

14. Where on the computer do you find the space bar and the shift key? *(Keyboard)*

15. Give the steps for exiting a program on the computer.

    (Use steps for your media center)

16. What dial controls the sound level on a piece of audiovisual equipment? *(Volume)*

17. Which one of these words would you look for to make the picture image on a screen clearer?   Focus or tilt.   *(Focus)*

18. True of False? You can look for audiovisual materials under the subject as well as the title in the computer catalog.   *(True)*

19. Make a statement that compares a globe to the Earth.

    (The globe is round like the Earth
    The globe spins like the Earth
    The globe is tilted like the Earth
    The globe shows the location of land and water areas
    The globe shows the locations of the major mountains and rivers of the Earth)

20. Tell a rule to follow in the computer lab.

    (Do not eat or drink in the computer lab.
    Do not remove diskettes while disk light is on.
    Wait for signal to turn the computer on and off.)

21. Tell a rule to follow in the media center.

    (Depends on the media center)

22. Tell the procedure to use to load a computer program.

    (Depends on the computer)

23. Tell where the various nonbook materials are in the media center.

    (Depends on the media center)

Questions 6 and 19–23 may be repeated. Direct students to provide another answer.

Seek and Find

Purpose

A board game or worksheet to review general media center questions.

To Make

Duplicate the Seek and Find puzzle shown on the next page on paper (one for each child) or on a posterboard .

To Play

Divide the class into two teams. Give the first player a clue to one of the words on the board (See examples). Direct that player to tell you what word you are hunting for and to point to that word on the board. If correct, give that team two points – one for the correct answer and one for locating the word on the board.

Follow the same procedure with a player from the next team and continue alternately asking questions until all the words have been found.

Paper Activity

Have students locate the words on the paper instead of the posterboard.

Seek & Find

	1	2	3	4	5	6	7	8	9	10	11
A	C	D	E	C	O	M	P	U	T	E	R
B	A	N	O	N	F	I	C	T	I	O	N
C	L	R	E	F	E	R	E	N	C	E	P
D	L	E	E	A	S	Y	B	O	O	K	U
E	N	C	X	I	N	D	E	X	P	S	B
F	U	T	I	T	L	E	S	C	Y	P	L
G	M	F	S	A	U	T	H	O	R	I	I
H	B	F	I	C	T	I	O	N	I	N	S
I	E	T	I	T	L	E	P	A	G	E	H
J	R	B	I	O	G	R	A	P	H	Y	E
K	I	L	L	U	S	T	R	A	T	O	R

Seek and Find Sample Questions

1. Who prints a book? *(C-11)*

2. What is a story that is created from someone's imagination? *(H-2)*

3. What is an alphabetical key to names, places, topics found in a book? *(E-4)*

4. In what section would an encyclopedia be found? *(C-2)*

5. Where can you find complete information about any material in the library? *(A-4 across)*

6. Where can you find the call numbers on a book? *(E-10)*

7. What is a storybook with mostly pictures? *(D-3)*

8. What is on the spine of a book that tells what section the book belongs to? *(A-1 down)*

9. Who does the pictures for a book? *(F-2)*

10. What is a book that is true called? *(B-2)*

11. What is the name of a book? *(F-2)*

12. What symbol means the book is legally protected? *(C-9)*

13. Who writes a book? *(G-4)*

14. What is a book about the life of a person called? *(J-2)*

15. Where can you find information on the author, title, or publisher in a book? *(I-2)*

16. What letters stand for compact disk? *(A-1)*

Additional questions

1. What is 629.1? *(A-1 down)*

2. What kind of book is *Charlotte's Web*? *(H-2)*

3. What is Abraham Lincoln? *(J-2)*

4. In what section would the atlas be found? *(C-2)*

5. What is Children's Press? *(C-11)*

6. What is 1982? *(C-9)*

42

Go Around the Alphabet

Purpose

To review locating authors' last names on sample title pages.

To Make

Write letters of the alphabet on the outer edge of a posterboard. Repeat some of the letters. Write the title in the center of the board. Put two clothespins at a designated starting point.

Make six cards with the word GO on each card.

Make 25 to 30 cards with sample title pages.

To Play

Divide the class into two teams. Direct the first player to draw a card and state the letter(s) the book would be alphabetized by on the shelves. Move a clip to that letter on the board. If the letter appears more than once on the board, go to the nearest one.

Follow the same procedure with a player from the other team. Continue the game until each student has had a turn. Each time a team passes the starting point, give a GO card.

The team with the most GO cards wins the game.

Game board

Sample title pages

Go cards

T.A.P.

Purpose

To review title page information.

To Make

Paste circles or other shapes around the edge of a posterboard as shown in the example. Shapes may be cut out of die cutters. Indicate a starting point and a shortcut path. Label the game T.A.P. Write fiction titles, authors' names, and publishers on the shapes. Use publishers' names that have words such as press, company, incorporated, or publishing company.

You will need a dice or a spinner and two clothespins or clips.

To Play

Divide the group into two teams. Direct the first player to throw the dice or spin the spinner. Move the clothespin or clamp the number of jumps indicated. The player tells whether the information on the shape the marker is on is a title, an author, or a publisher. If correct the marker is not moved. If incorrect the marker is moved back to the starting point.

Continue with a player from the other team. If that team lands on the same shape that has been correctly identified, give information from the title page of a book. Alternate players and move until one team reaches the end point.

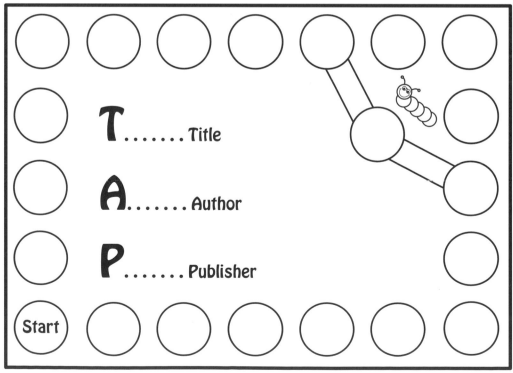

Game board

Parts of a Book Bingo

Purpose

To review book terms and book parts.

To Make

Duplicate and give each student a copy of the Bingo sheet on the next page. Direct the students to write one word in each of their Bingo squares. You may use just the words below or add other terms you wish to review. Have each student create their own Bingo card, encouraging them to use some words more than once in order to make unique cards.

author	illustrator	spine
title	glossary	copyright date
index	publisher	place of publication

Write on small cards specific authors' names, titles, publishers, etc. For illustrators, put such words as: pictures by, illustrated by, with drawings by. For the word "spine," ask questions such as:

What is found on the bottom of the spine? *call number*

How are nonfiction spines arranged? *number order*

For glossary and index, ask the definitions of these words and where they are located in the book.

To Play

Draw a card and call out the information. Direct the students to mark on the upper left-hand corner of the block that answers the information given—one block per card e.g., Children's Press — publisher).

Continue the game with the students marking the upper left-hand corners for the first game. Play until someone gets a Bingo or three marks in a row.

For the next games, have students use the upper right-hand corners for the second game, the bottom left-hand corners for the third game, and the bottom right-hand corners for the fourth game. Use the center for the final, fifth game.

Parts of a Book Bingo

Write these words in the blocks below. Use only one word per block. You may use some of the words more than one time. Do not write these words in the exact order as listed on this page.

AUTHOR	**COPYRIGHT DATE**	**SPINE**
TITLE	**ILLUSTRATOR**	**GLOSSARY**
PUBLISHER	**INDEX**	**PLACE OF PUBLICATION**

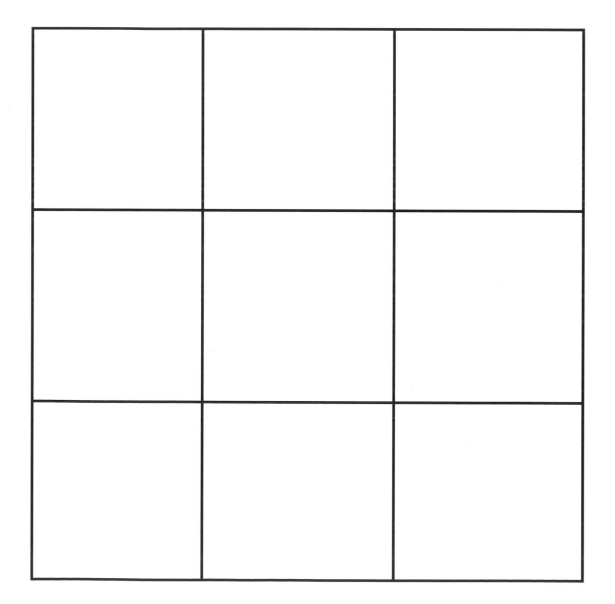

Shape-Up

Purpose

To review parts of a book.

To Make

Cut 21 circles, triangles and squares (seven of each) from brightly colored paper. *(See next page for patterns.)* Print each of the words below on each of the shapes (once on a circle, once on a square, and once on a triangle). Or substitute other words pertaining to parts of a book you prefer to reinforce.

spine	*glossary*	*title page*	*contents*
index	*foreword*	*bibliography*	

Arrange the shapes on a posterboard that is at least 20x26", leaving room for the game title. Tape an edge of each shape to the board, making it a flap. Trace around each shape with a black marker. Under each flap, print a point value (5, 10, or 25) at random.

Prepare a set of questions that are "answered" by one of the terms you have selected for the Shape-Up board. You will need to create several for each word. *(See the sample list following the pattern page.)*

To Play

Divide the class into two teams. Begin by reading the first question and having the player try to identify the shape word it matches. Upon answering correctly, the player selects one of the three shapes corresponding to that word and lifts its flap, receiving the points indicated on the game board for the team. Continue by asking the next question of the opposing team.

If answered incorrectly, the opposing team is given the opportunity to answer. The team with the most points wins.

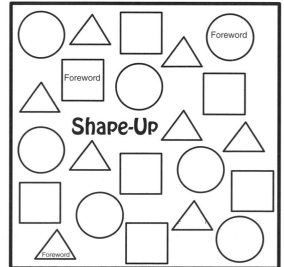

Game board

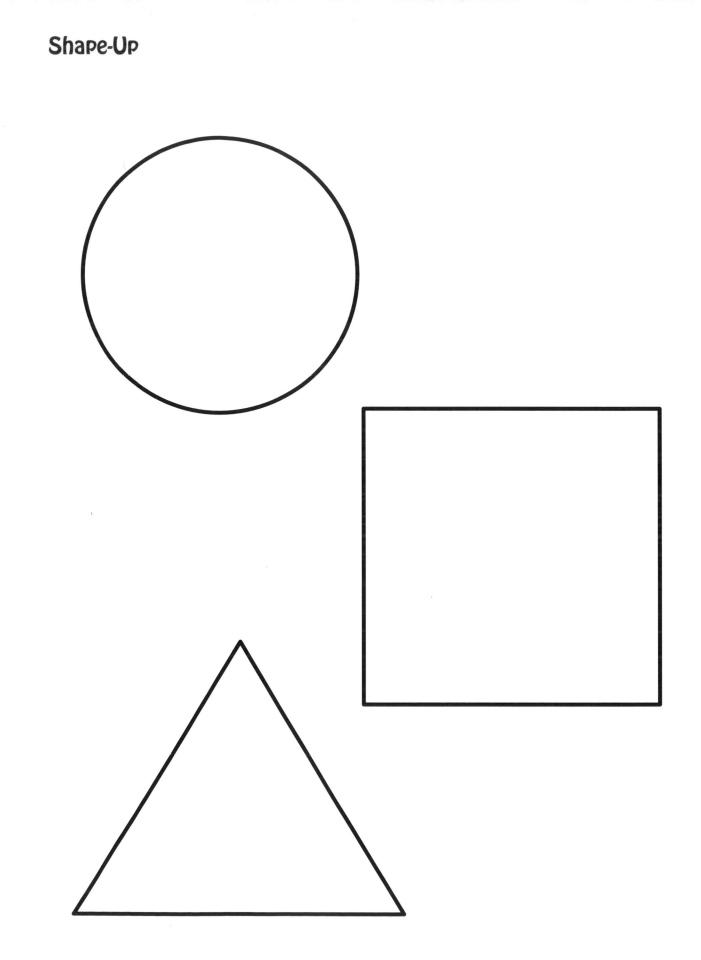

Questions for Shape-Up

Where can this information be found?

A list of new or difficult words and their meanings. *(Glossary)*

Information about the publisher, author, title. *(Title page)*

A list of the page numbers where all the chapters begin. *(Contents)*

A statement by the author about why he or she wrote the book. *(Foreword)*

An alphabetical list with page numbers where a particular subject may be found. *(Index)*

A list of books that are all about one subject. *(Bibliography)*

Call numbers. *(Spine)*

A list of other titles by an author. *(Bibliography)*

The title of all the chapters in the book. *(Contents)*

An introduction to this book. *(Foreword)*

The copyright date. *(Title page)*

What is this called?

Where the pages of a book are sewn together. *(Spine)*

One of the items that appears in the back of a book. *(Index, glossary)*

One of the items that appears in the front of the book. *(Title page, contents, foreword)*

Grades 3–5

Cube 'N' Cards

Purpose

To review identification of title page and other basic publishing information.

To Make

Cover a large square box with construction paper. Write these words on the sides of the box (each side one word):

| TITLE | ILLUSTRATOR | COPYRIGHT DATE |
| AUTHOR | PUBLISHER | CALL NUMBER |

Create a set of game cards on index cards. Write a specific example for one of the title page words above on each card. For example, your set of author cards might include Judy Blume, Sid Fleischman, Jane Yolen, Laura Wilder, etc. *(See examples on the next page or use the optional directions below.)*

To Play

Divide the class into two teams. Divide the cards into two equal stacks and give them to the teams. Start the game by directing a player to toss the cube. Ask that team to give you a card that corresponds with the word that is face up on the cube (e.g., Beverly Cleary for the word AUTHOR). Accept only one card each time.

Optional: Have students find title pages and point to the appropriate information. If the information given does not correspond correctly with the word, return the card and ask the other team to give up one of its cards with the correct information as a bonus.

Follow the same procedure with the other team and continue the game until you have collected most of the cards. The team with the fewest cards left wins the game.

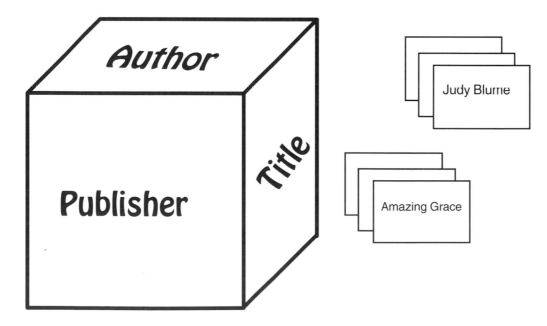

Sample Cards for Cube 'N' Card Game

James Howe

Amazing Grace

629.1
Col

Miss Nelson Is Missing

Lois Lowry

Orchard Books

©1991

Macmillan Press

©1996

Pictures by Paul Brett Johnson

Scott, Foresman & Company

Houghton Mifflin Company

B
Lin

CLE

Dial Books

Thomas Rockwell

The Giver

©1989

Illustrated by Maurice Sendak

Wayside School Is Falling Down

Random House, Inc.

Jean George

Pictures by Donald Crews

Up and Away with Books

Purpose

To review information found on the title page

To Make

Take about six title pages from discarded books (or copy and enlarge pages from books) and attach with rings to a posterboard.

Write the words, author, title, illustrator, and publisher (one word per card) on 3x5" cards. Make only about twelve cards, as these can be shuffled and used again.

On another posterboard, tape at least ten balloon flaps and write 5,10, or 15 underneath the flaps. The two boards may be hinged or used separately.

To Play

Divide the class into two teams. Direct the first player to draw a question card. Have that player identify on the title page by reading or pointing the information that corresponds to the word on the question card. If correct, have the player pick a balloon to see how many points that person has earned for his team. If incorrect, no points are given.

The other team follows the same procedure and the game continues until all have had a turn. Add up the score and the team with the most points wins.

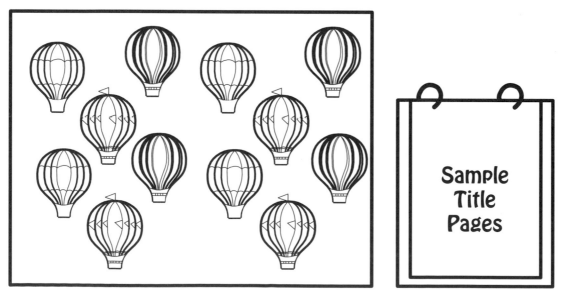

Game board

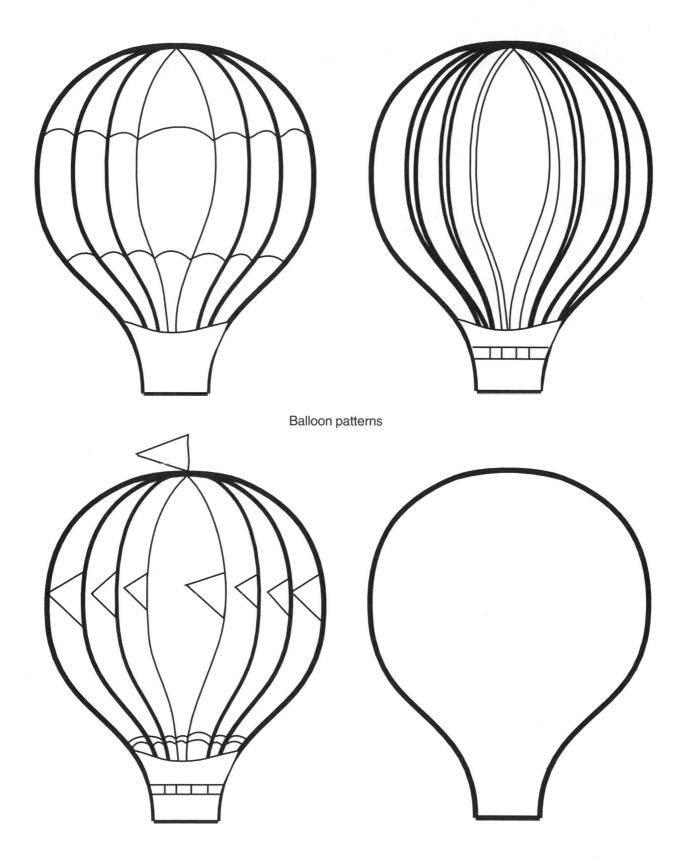

Balloon patterns

Title Page Express

Purpose

To review title and copyright page information.

To Make

Use the patterns to make a train out of construction paper. Cut out a train car for each item listed below. Decorate the train cars and paste them on a posterboard. Tape picture hangers on the cars.

Make about ten sets of title page samples on 3x5" index cards. Then on separate cards, write the specific titles, authors, illustrators, publishers and copyright dates from the corresponding title page, each on a separate card. Punch holes at the top center of the cards.

To Play

Divide the class into two teams. Give a player from the first team a set of cards (title page card and matching set). Direct the player to put the cards on the hangers. Give a point for each correct answer. Follow the same procedure with the other team and continue alternating turns until the cards have all been used. The team with the most points wins the game.

This game idea can also be used with card or OPAC catalog information.

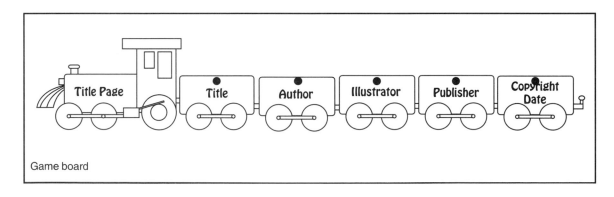

Game board

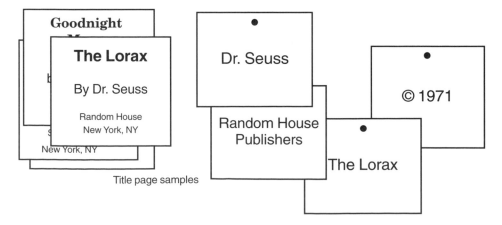

Title page samples

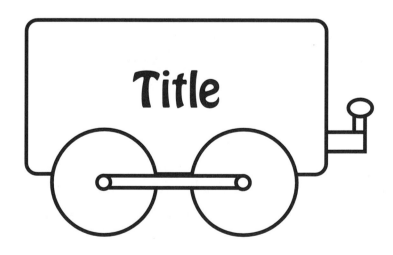

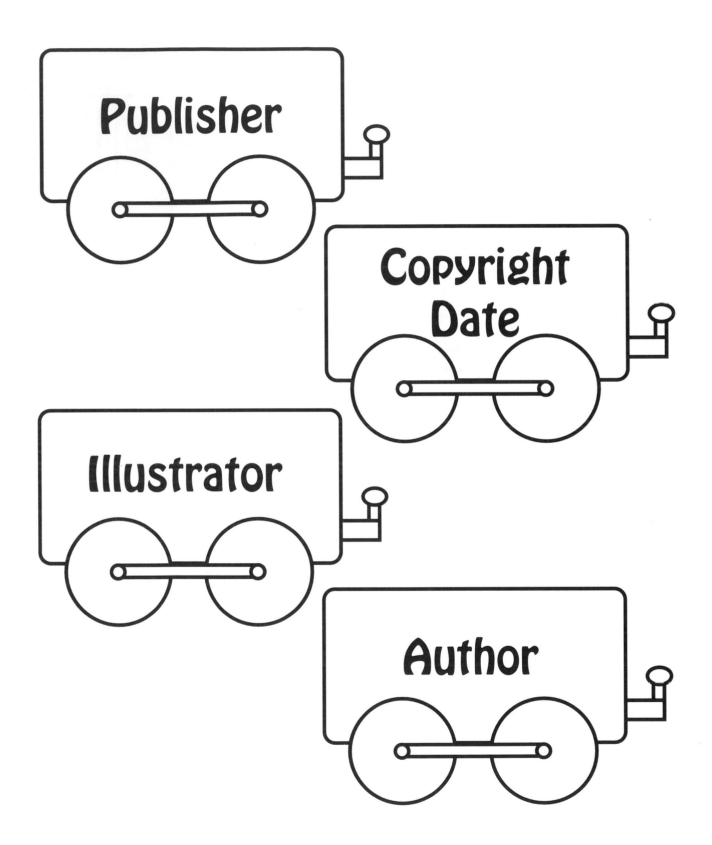

Decisions, Decisions

Purpose

To review skills related to books.

To Make

Write true or false statements related to books on at least 30 3x5" index cards. *(See examples on next page.)*

Using 10 new cards write:

Take 1 (4 cards)

Take 2 (3 cards)

Take 3 (2 cards)

Take 4 (1 card)

To Play

Divide the class into two teams. Make two stacks of cards: Question cards and Take cards. Direct each team to send one player to draw cards for the team. These players will draw the cards for the entire game. Direct the first player to draw a "Take" card. Then have the player take as many question cards as indicated on the "Take" card. Read these cards to that player's team and have team members answer with a true or false answer. If an answer is correct, the team can claim the card. If not, the card is tossed out.

Continue the same procedure with the other team and play the game until the question cards are all gone. The team with the most cards wins the game.

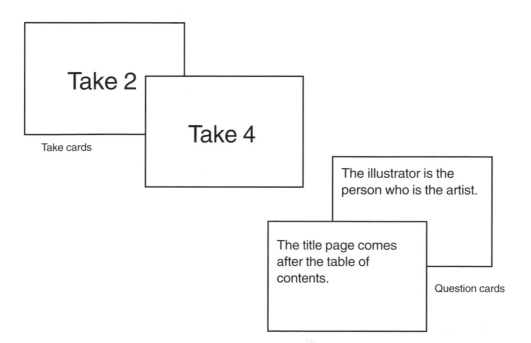

Take 2

Take cards

Take 4

The illustrator is the person who is the artist.

The title page comes after the table of contents.

Question cards

Decisions, Decisions Questions

True or False Statements:

1. Words in the index are listed in alphabetical order.

2. The spine of the book has the illustrator's name.

3. Chapters or stories listed in the table of contents are in alphabetical order.

4. The title page comes after the table of contents.

5. Words listed in the index have page numbers.

6. You will find the illustrator's name on the title page.

7. The title page has page numbers.

8. The spine of the book has call numbers on it.

9. The table of contents has page numbers.

10. You will find the publisher's name in the table of contents page.

11. The title information is usually at the bottom of the title page.

12. You can find the publisher information on the top of the title page.

13. The author and the illustrator are found in the middle of the title page.

14. You can find the table of contents at the back of the book.

15. The catalog in the computer can be arranged in alphabetical order.

16. A magazine is a periodical because it is printed in regular time periods.

17. Fiction books are shelved in number order.

18. Nonfiction books are shelved by the authors' names.

19. The illustrator is the person who is the artist.

20. The publisher is the person who wrote the book.

21. The copyright date is found on the spine of the book.

22. *Ranger Rick* is a periodical.

23. The computer catalog does not have the call numbers of the books.

25. Biographies are shelved in number order.

26. The three letters under the B of biography come from the author's last name.

27. A fiction call number has three letters from the author's last name.

28. Nonfiction books are shelved according to subjects or to what they are about.

29. Nonfiction books are books of fact, not fantasy.

30. A biography is a book about the life of a person, living or not.

Castles and Creatures

Purpose

To review title page information. Also can be used with other skills.

To Make

Draw or paste pictures of trees along the edge of a large posterboard. Draw or paste on a pond, a dragon, a bear, and a castle. *(See patterns on p. 61.)*

You will need two clothespins to mark the moves along the board.

Write the questions *(See examples on pp. 62–63.)* and the number of moves on 30 or more cards. Make several Golden Key and Dragon questions.

To Play

Divide the class into two teams. Separate the Golden Key and Dragon questions and keep them in a separate stack. Direct the first player to draw a card, read the question, and answer it. If the answer is correct, move according to the number of moves indicated on the back of the card. Move the clothespin, large clip or clamp on the trees, each tree is a space. If the answer is incorrect, the team does not get to move.

On the last move before entering the castle, a player must answer a Golden Key question. If the answer is correct, that team gets to enter the castle and win the game. If incorrect, the team must try again on their next turn.

Castles and Creatures Game Rules

Pond: Lose a turn. If you have a Magic Bridge card, advance one.

Dragon Space: Answer a question from the Dragon Card deck. If the answer is correct, the player can go on to the next space. If incorrect, the player must retreat three spaces. If the player lands on a Bear space, he must retreat one space.

Shortcut: If you land on this space, cut across the trees.

Bear: Retreat two spaces unless you have a Magic Sword card.

Golden Key: Before you enter the castle, you must answer a Golden Key question. If incorrect, wait for another turn to try again.

Castles and Creatures

Start

Golden Key
Question

Castles
and
Creatures

Pond

Bear

Dragon

Shortcut

Game board

60

Castles and Creatures Questions

Front of card: **Back of card:**

1. Is the title page before or after the contents page?   *before (move 1)*

2. Is the publisher usually found at the top, middle or bottom of
   the title page ?   *bottom (move 1)*

3. Are the author and the illustrator found at the top, middle or
   bottom of the title page?   *middle (move 1)*

4. True or false? The index is found before the table of contents.   *false (move 1)*

5. © stands for _____.   *copyright (move 3)*

6. Author, title, or publisher? Orchard Books   *publisher (move 2)*

7. Illustrator or publisher? Pictures by _____.   *illustrator (move 2)*

8. What information follows the word by on the title page?   *author (move 1)*

9. You found a Magic Sword. Keep the sword. If you land on the
   Dragon or Bear spaces, advance by 1 extra jump.
   (Make two of these cards)

10. You found a Magic Bridge to go over the Enchanted Pond.
    Save this magic. If you should land on the Pond, use this to
    advance by one extra jump.

11. What does an illustrator do for a book?   *pictures (move 1)*

12. Where is the title usually found on the title page?   *top (move 1)*

13. If the copyright date is not on the front of the title page,
    where can it be found?   *back of title page
                                                                             (move 2)*

14. What information is this? *A Wrinkle in Time*   *title (move 1)*

15. True or false? The Table of Contents is at the back of the book.   *false (move 1)*

Golden Key Questions

1. Give an example of a title.
2. Give an example of a fiction title.
3. Give an example of a biography title.
4. Give an example of a nonfiction title.
5. Give an example of an author.

Dragon Questions

1. Where are the fiction books in the library?

   Advance 1 if correct.

   Retreat 3 if incorrect.

2. Where are the nonfiction books in the library?

   Advance 1 if correct.

   Retreat 3 if incorrect.

3. Where are the biographies in the library?

   Advance 1 if correct.

   Retreat 3 if incorrect.

4. Where are the nonfiction materials in the library?

   Advance 1 if correct.

   Retreat 3 if incorrect

5. Where are the reference books in the library?

   Advance 1 if correct

   Retreat 3 if incorrect

Memory Game

Purpose

To review call numbers.

To Make

On a posterboard, tape an even-number of flaps and write numbers on the flaps as shown below. Paste pockets underneath the flaps.

Cut cards to fit into the pockets you have created so that the card will stay securely in the pocket and the word or letters you have written on it can still be easily read by students.

You can also match authors' names to their call numbers.

Randomly place the cards into the pockets.

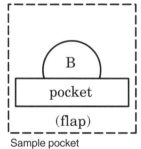

Sample pocket

To Play

Divide the class into two teams. Direct each student to come up and lift two flaps. If the cards match, give that team a point for the match and a second point for answering a question about the call number (e.g., Define biography or Where are biographies located?).

As matches are found, remove the cards from the pockets. If all matches are found before each student has had a turn, shuffle cards and put them back under the flaps. The team with the most points wins the game.

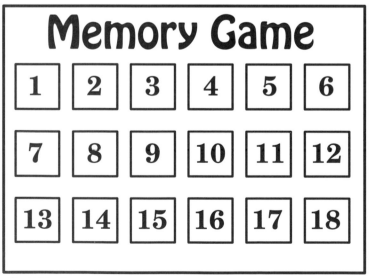

Game board

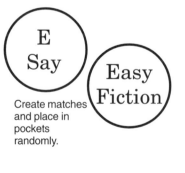

Create matches and place in pockets randomly.

Sample Matches:

B	BIOGRAPHY
Numbers	NONFICTION
E three letters	EASY FICTION
SC	STORY COLLECTION

Match Maker

Purpose

To teach and/or reinforce call numbers.

To Make

Paste fifteen library pockets on a posterboard. Label the pockets with call numbers that reinforce the recognition you want emphasized. Title the board.

On small cards (3x5"), type statements that match the call numbers. The samples on the next page fit the group of call numbers shown below.

To Play

Individual students select a statement card and, after determining the matching call number, place the card in the correct pocket.

Teams could be selected and a score recorded, but it may be more advantageous just to use this activity as a point of discussion.

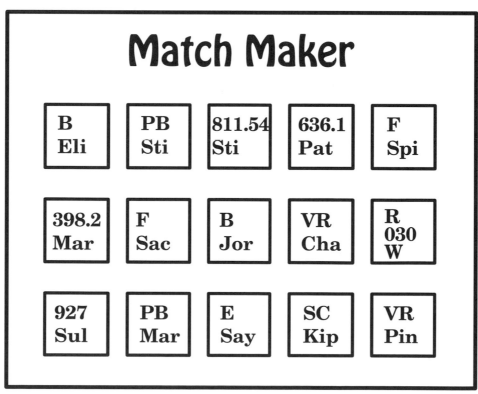

Game board

Cards for Match-Maker

B
Eli   The life of Queen Elizabeth

PB
Mar   A paperback. Baby-Sitters Club book by Ann M. Martin

VR
Cha   A video of *Charlotte's Web* by E.B. White

F
Sac   A Wayside School story by Louis Sachar

VR
Pln   A video-recording of *Pinocchio*

F
Spi   The book *Maniac Magee* by Jerry Spinelli

B
Jor   A true story about Michael Jordan

636.1
Pat   A book of information about horses

R
030
Wor   *World Book Encyclopedia*

SC
Kip   The *Just So Stories* by Rudyard Kipling

E
Say   A picture book by Allan Say

811.54
Sil   The book of poems, *A Light in the Attic*, by Shel Silverstein

PB
Sti   A paperback book by R.L. Stine

927
Sul   The book *Sluggers* about 27 baseball players by George Sullivan

398.2
Mar   The folktale *The Rough-Face Girl* by Rafe Martin

Red Light, Green Light

Purpose

A drill-like activity to review call numbers or information on a title page or catalog screen or card.

To Make

Draw three circles on each of 37 4x6" index cards. *(See samples on next page.)* Color the top circles red on seven cards. Color the bottom circles green on 30 cards. In the center circles of the green cards write:

Call Numbers

- Fiction and nonfiction call numbers for 1st and 2nd grades.
- Fiction, nonfiction, and biography call numbers for 3rd grades.
- Nonbook and all types of book call numbers for 4th and 5th grades.

Title Page Information

- Authors and titles for 1st grades.
- Authors, titles, and illustrators for 2nd grades (Use word clues as drawings by; pictures by; illustrated by, for illustrator information.
- Authors, titles, illustrators, and publishers for grades 3–5.

Catalog Information

- Authors, titles, publishers, subjects or key words (written in all capital letters), copyright dates, call numbers, number of pages.

To Play

Divide the class into two teams. "Stack the deck" of cards so there are four green cards to the fifth red card. Direct one team player to identify the information in the center circle of a green card, one person per card. As long as the answer is correct, that team claims that card. If incorrect, the card is tossed out. The team continues as long as the cards are green. When the red light appears, the other side takes over. The side with the most cards wins the game.

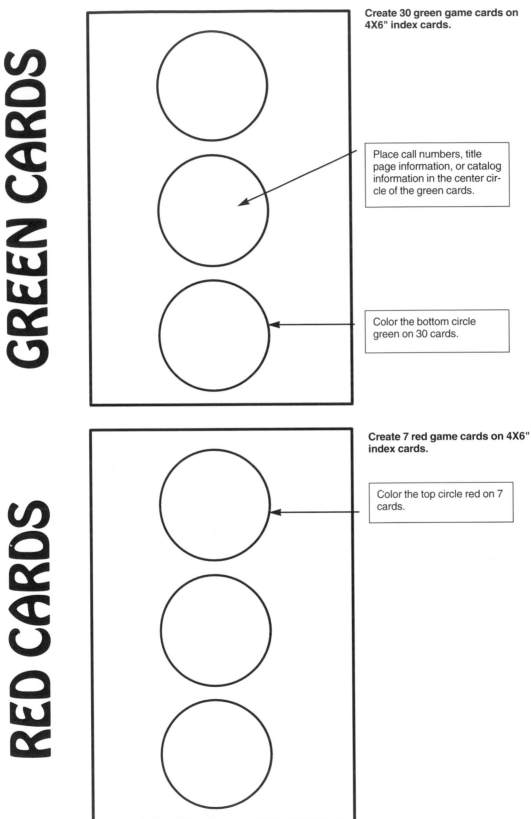

GREEN CARDS

Create 30 green game cards on 4X6" index cards.

Place call numbers, title page information, or catalog information in the center circle of the green cards.

Color the bottom circle green on 30 cards.

RED CARDS

Create 7 red game cards on 4X6" index cards.

Color the top circle red on 7 cards.

Call Number Catch

Purpose

To give students practice in identifying call numbers.

To Make

Duplicate the pictures of sea animals from the following pages. Cut out about 25 to 30 animals and put brads or paper clips on them. Write fiction and nonfiction call numbers on them for grades 1 and 2 and add biography call numbers for grade 3. Tie a magnet to a string and tie the string to a long stick. Put the sea animals in a cardboard carton.

To Play

Divide the class into two teams. Give each student a turn to come up to "fish." When that student catches a fish, have him identify whether the call number on the fish is fiction, nonfiction, or biography (grade 3).

If correct, that team claims that catch. If not, the fish "got away." At the end of the class period, count the catch (one point per animal). You can designate points for the type of catch (e.g., 1 for turtle; 5 for whale). The team with the most points wins the game.

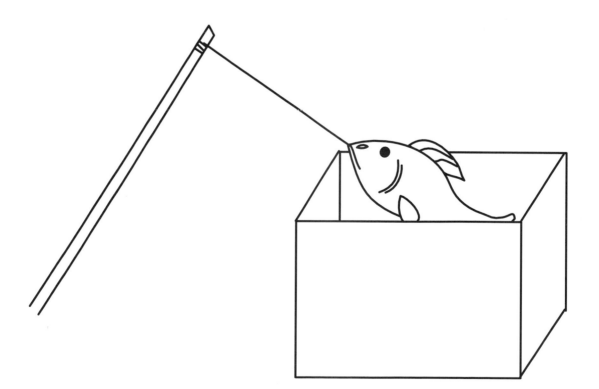

Call Number Catch

Grades 3–5

Call Number Scramble

Purpose

To provide students with practice putting fiction, nonfiction, or biography call numbers in order.

To Make

Make several sets of game cards by writing either fiction, nonfiction, or biography call numbers on 3x5" index cards (10 cards per set). Do not mix the fiction call numbers with the nonfiction or biography sets (and vice versa).

You will need a pocket chart (shown below) and a stopwatch.

To Play

Divide the class into two teams. Have two players from one team come up and put the call numbers from one set in order on the pocket chart. Time how long it takes them to get all ten cards in order. Continue by having the next team do the same thing with another set of cards. Switch back to the first team, using a different set of call numbers. At the completion of the races, add up the time. The team with the lowest time wins.

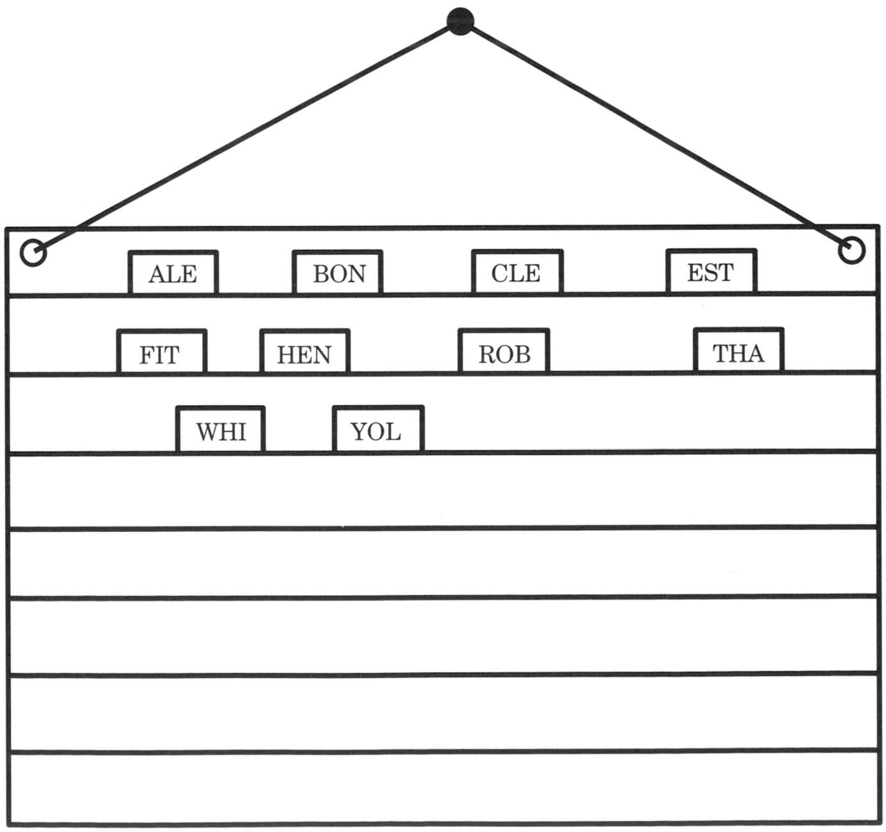

ALE   BON   CLE   EST

FIT   HEN   ROB   THA

WHI   YOL

Pocket chart

Run for the Shelves

Purpose

To provide a practice activity for students to locate particular call numbers at the shelves.

To Make

You will need six cards for each type of race. You will also need a stopwatch.

On the 3x5" cards write:

- First letters of fiction call numbers for grades 1–2.

- First and second letters of fiction call numbers for grades 2–3.

- Fiction call numbers for grades 3–5.

- First number of nonfiction call numbers for grades 2–3.

- First and second numbers of nonfiction call numbers for grades 3–4.

- Nonfiction call numbers for grades 4–6.

(Make six cards for each set)

To Play

Divide the class into equal teams (about four or five students per team). Give the set of six cards to the first team. Be sure to give only call numbers of books you know are on the shelves. Give a signal for that team to go to the shelves to place cards beside the books with those call numbers.

Time how long it takes the team to complete the task. Take the cards out of the shelves and repeat the procedure with the next team. The team with the lowest time wins the race.

Nailing Nonfiction

Purpose

To review the Dewey Decimal Classification System.

To Make

Cut a large house shape out of posterboard. Paste ten pockets on the posterboard. Cut and paste ten pictures of tools on the outside of the pockets.

Take 20 3x5" cards and paste one tool image on each, so that you have two per tool. Write two questions for each of the tools so that you have a different question for each team. Put these cards in the appropriate pockets. *(See sample questions on p. 76.)*

To Play

Tell students that the object of this game is to collect all the necessary tools to build a house. The first team to collect all ten items wins the game.

Divide the class into two teams. Have the first player pick a tool he would like. Read a question from that tool card. If that player answers correctly, give the tool to that team. If not, put the tool card back in the pocket. Follow the same procedure with a player from the other team and continue the game, alternating turns until one side gets all ten tools and is declared the winner.

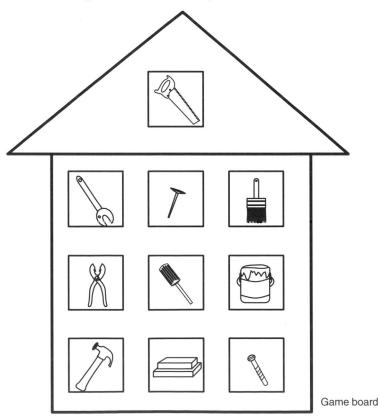

Game board

Nailing Nonfiction Sample Questions

1. How many major sections are nonfiction books divided into?

   a. 5   b.10   c.15

2. The numbering system nonfiction books are divided into is called the _____ Decimal Classification System.

   a. Caldecott   b. Newbery   c. Dewey

3. Where are the nonfiction books?

4. Which of these subjects does not belong to the natural science or 500 section?

   a. trees   b. transportation   c. turtles

5. Which of these call numbers does not belong to the 500 section?

   a. 598.1   b. 512   c. 915

6. Which of these call numbers comes first in the 500 section?

   a. 595   b. 568.1   c. 523.3

7. Tell me an example of a book in the 500 or natural science section.

8. Does the 500 section come at the beginning, middle, or end of the nonfiction section?

9. Hand me a book from the 500 section.

10. Put a book back from the 500 section.

11. Find a dinosaur book that has the call number 568.

Continue with similar questions for other nonfiction sections.

A Class Act

Purpose

To review the Dewey Decimal Classification System.

To Make

Create a subject list, twenty per group, for the 500s, 600s, 700s, or 900s. You can duplicate this list for each student or you can write these subjects on a board for general review.

Write each of these subjects on a on a 3x6" card. Place ten cards from one group backward on a pocket chart.

To Play

Review the Dewey Decimal Classification System and the subject terms either from sheets or on the board. After the review, you will need to make sure students cannot see this list.

Divide the class into two teams. Direct the starting team to name ten subjects in the 500 category. Write these on a chalkboard. Then turn over the ten cards you placed in the pocket chart. Give that team points for each word they have matched (i.e., subject on card matches subject on chalkboard). Shuffle cards and place ten (out of the twenty) backward on the board and continue same procedure with the other team.

Switch to the 600s and let the second team start this time. Tally the score and the team with the most points wins the game.

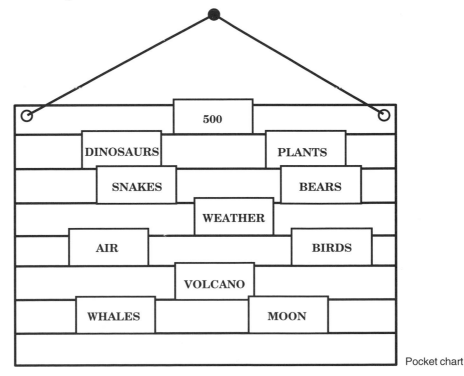

Pocket chart

S.A.T.

Purpose

To review three ways of hunting for information in a library computer catalog.

To Make

Draw blocks around a posterboard. In the blocks write subjects and key words (in capital letters), authors (last name first), and titles (capitalize just the first letter of the title). Cut the letters S, A and T out of construction paper and paste them in the center of the board.

Prepare a list of extra authors, titles, and subjects. You will also need a cube or spinner and two clothespins, large clips or clamps to play this game.

To Play

Divide the class into two teams. Direct the first player to throw the cube or spin the spinner. Move one of the clips the appropriate number of jumps. Have that player identify whether the information in the block is an author, title, or subject. If the answer is correct, leave the clip there. If incorrect, move back to where it was. Follow the same procedure with the other team. If a team lands on a block that has been correctly identified, give an entry from your extra list.

Continue alternating turns until one team reaches the starting position and is declared the winner.

Shiloh	POETRY	*The River*	MYTHS	Cooper, Susan	BASEBALL	*Beanpole*
Indian in the Cupboard						MAGIC
Sobol, Donald		S......Subject				Hamilton, Virginia
Howliday Inn		A......Author				*Trouble with Tuck*
Dahl, Roald		T......Title				WATER
START	*Dear Mr. Henshaw*	George, Jean	KARATE	Blume, Judy	*The Westing Game*	*Toad for Tuesday*

Game board

Cruising the Catalog

Purpose

To review information in a computer catalog .

To Make

Cut a large circle out of posterboard or get a large pizza board. Draw about 30–32 segments on the board. *(See sample on the next page.)* Each segment should contain a word or words that relate to a type of catalog information and a number that indicates the spaces a player can move. One segment is reserved for START/FINISH and five segments should be marked as BONUS squares. Other segments can be labeled as follows:

Author 1	*Copyright date 2*	*BONUS*
Title 1	*Number of pages 1*	*START/ FINISH*
Publisher 3	*Call number 2*	
Subject 3	*Illustrator 3*	

Repeat each catalog term about three times.

You will need a number spinner or a cube and two clothespins or clips.

Either duplicate several pages of sample computer information to be given to each player or make large ones to be seen by the entire group.

> AUTHOR 1) Hamilton, Virginia
>
> TITLE   The planet of Junior Brown.
>
> PUBLISHER   New York, Macmillan [1971]
>
> DESCRIPTIO   210 p. 22 cm.
>
> SUBJECTS   l) Afro-Americans -- Social conditions --
> Juvenile fiction   2) Friendship -- Juvenile fiction
>
>   Press <Enter> to see next screen :
>
> SO=Start Over, B=Back, RW=Related Works,

Sample catalog data

To Play

Divide the class into two teams. To get the game started, direct the first player to spin the spinner or throw the cube. Move the clip the appropriate number of jumps along the edge of the board. Tell the player to use the sample catalog pages to give you information that corresponds to the word shown on the segment the clip landed on. If the information is correct, move the clip again according to the number shown on the segment. However, that player does not answer again. If incorrect, move back to starting segment. Continue the same procedure with a player from the other team. If the team lands on BONUS, spin the spinner or throw the cube for extra jumps.

To continue the game, have each player begin their turn by giving the catalog example for the segment their team is currently on. If correct, they may then move the designated number of jumps. Leaving the team marker on the new square where their teammate will take it over on the next turn. The first to get to FINISH wins the game.

Cruising 'Round the Catalog

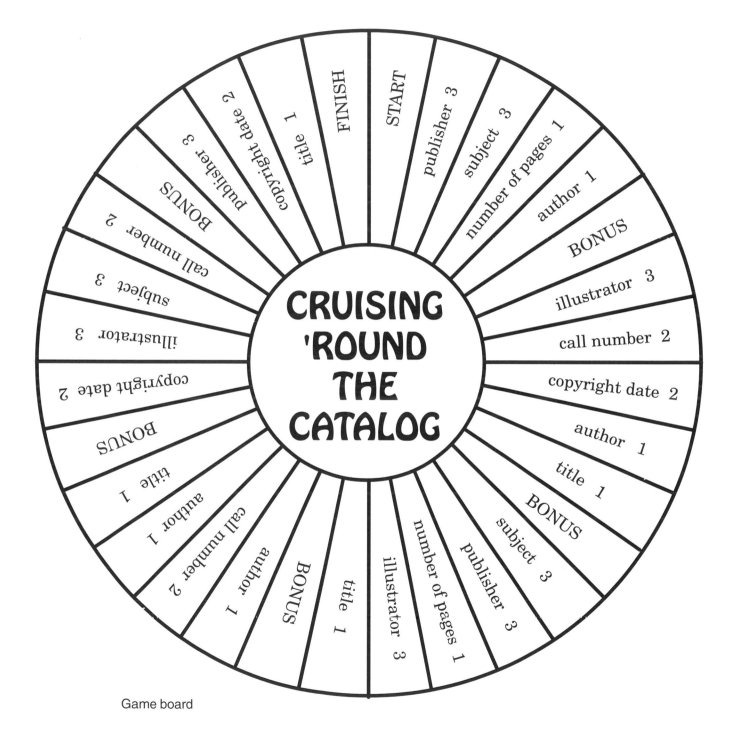

Game board

Aliens Attack

Purpose

To review computer catalog information.

To Make

Tape twelve slots on a posterboard *(shown on the next page)*. Hinge this board to another board. Draw five vertical lines over the slots.

Use the space ship patterns to make twelve Alien ships and two Defender ships. Write 1 and 2 on the Defender ships and the letters for ALIENS ATTACK on the Alien ships (one letter per ship).

Make large samples of catalog information and attach with rings to the second board.

On 3x5" index cards, write (one item per card):

Move 1	Aliens Retreat 1
Fire 1	Aliens Advance 1
Move 1, Fire 1	Move 2
Move 1, 2, or 3, Fire 1	

Make another set of cards using these words (one item per card):

Author	Call Number	Subject
Title	Number of Pages	Copyright Date
Publisher	Illustrator	

To Play

Divide the class into two teams. Designate which team will be Defender 1 and which team will be Defender 2. Place Defender 1 on the first slot, right-hand side of the board. Place Defender 2 on the seventh slot, right-hand side of the board. Place the twelve Alien ships on the left-hand side of the board (one ship per slot).

Tell the students that the object of the game is to destroy the six alien ships on their half of the board. Defender 1 defends the top six slots; Defender 2 defends the bottom six slots.

The Defender ships can only move up and down. A **Fire 1** card results in a direct hit as long as the Alien ship is directly in line, a straight line that is, from the Defender ship. Remove Alien ships that have been successfully fired on.

Direct the first player to draw a question card and point to the corresponding information on the sample catalog entry. If correct, have that player draw a second card to determine the move on the board. If it is a "**Move**," move the Defender up or down in the six spaces. If it is a "Fire," it is a direct hit if there is an Alien in a straight path.

If the player answers incorrectly, move all six (or all remaining) Aliens forward one jump. If the Aliens reach a Defender ship the game is over and the other team is declared the winner. If the card drawn says **Aliens Retreat 1**, move back all of the Alien ships.

Alternate turns and follow the same procedure until one team destroys all six of the Alien ships on its side or a Defender ship is destroyed.

Aliens Attack

Place several samples from the online catalog here that illustrate the terms you have chosen for the game cards.

Alien ship

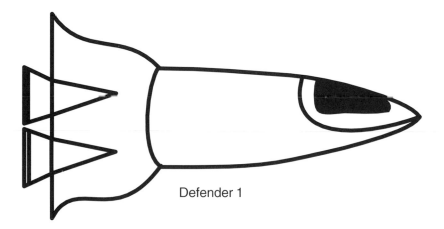

Defender 1

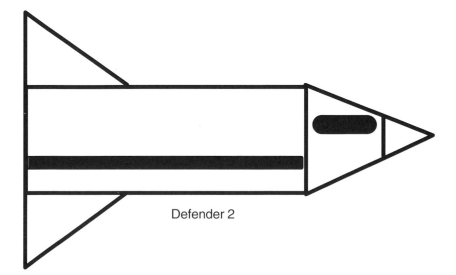

Defender 2

Reference Safari

Purpose

To review reference sources.

To Make

Reproduce the animals on the following pages. Paste them on a posterboard. Cut out flaps and tape over the rectangular shapes.

Write these words under the flaps:

Periodicals	**Unabridged dictionary**
Biographical dictionary	**Computer catalog**
Atlas	**Almanac**
Reference	**Nonfiction**
Encyclopedia	**Electronic Encyclopedia**
***Guinness Book of World Records* (optional)**	

To Play

Divide the class into two teams. Lift up all the flaps and read the hidden words. Close the flaps.

Give the first player a question *(see sample questions)*. Direct the player to tell you which animal has the correct answer. Lift the flap. If correct, give the team a point. Continue the same procedure with a player from the other team. The team with the most points wins the game.

Optional: You can also give a point to the player for correctly answering the question prior to locating the correct answer on the board.

Game board

Reference Safari Questions

1. What is a book of maps? *(Atlas)*

2. What has information on people, places, and events? *(Electronic encyclopedia; Encyclopedia)*

3. What is the symbol for a reference book? *(R)*

4. What is the section called that includes atlases, almanacs, and encyclopedias? *(Reference)*

5. What is a dictionary of people called? *(Biographical dictionary)*

6. What reference book has current information on people, places, and events? *(Almanac)*

7. What kind of books are reference books? *(Nonfiction)*

8. Where can you find information about the various reference books in the library? *(Card catalog, Online catalog)*

9. What is published at a regular interval and may have information on current topics? *(Magazines and periodicals)*

10. What includes almost all of the words of the English language? *(Unabridged dictionary)*

11. What reference book would have information on last year's World Series? *(Almanac)*

12. Which reference book would you use to write a report on Abraham Lincoln? *(Encyclopedia, Electronic encyclopedia)*

13. What reference book would you use to find the correct spelling of the word poltergeist? *(Unabridged dictionary)*

14. What reference help would you use if you needed to write a bibliography for your report on planets? *(Card catalog, Online catalog)*

15. Which reference book would help you locate the states that border Canada? *(Atlas)*

16. What reference book would you use to locate the states the Rocky Mountains are in? *(Atlas)*

17. What reference book would have information on flags? *(Electronic encyclopedia, Encyclopedia)*

18. What section of the library would have an index of poems? *(Reference)*

19. If you cannot locate information on a certain person in an encyclopedia, what other reference book may help?   *(Biographical dictionary)*

20. What reference book would have the names of the oldest living persons in the world?   *(Guinness Book of World Records)*

21. What reference book lists the present governors of each state?   *(Almanac)*

22. What reference book would have synonyms of words? *(Unabridged dictionary)*

23. Most reference books have numbers as call numbers. That means that most of them are _____.   *(Nonfiction)*

24. What are *National Geographic* and *National Geographic World*?   *(Periodicals)*

25. Where can you find information on whether the media center has any nonbook resources on ecology?   *(Card catalog, online catalog)*

26. What reference book would have the Olympic record in skiing?   *(Guinness Book of World Records)*

27. Which one of these would not have entries?   Encyclopedia   Nonfiction   Dictionary   *(Nonfiction)*

28. Which reference book would you use to report on unusual weather records?   *(Guinness Book of World Records)*

29. Which of these would you receive monthly?
Periodicals; Biographical dictionary   *(Periodicals)*

30. Which of these books would have information on Abraham Lincoln's wife Mary Todd Lincoln?   Unabridged dictionary; Biographical dictionary   *(Biographical dictionary)*

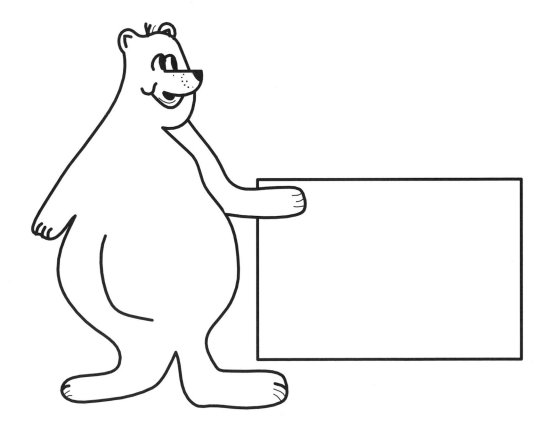

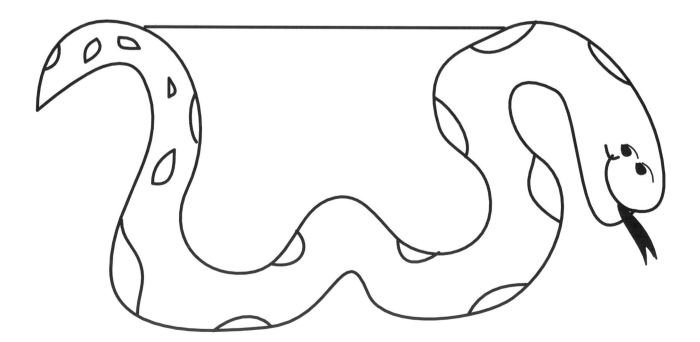

What Is It?

Purpose

An alphabetizing review and look-for-meaning activity.

To Make

A dictionary sheet for each student. *(See sample on the next page.)*

Each student will need a dictionary. Make sure the words you have selected can be found.

To Do

Students look up each word in the list, decide its category, and enter the word in the correct column. There are ten words for each topic. This activity may require two class periods. To conclude, go over the list with the class, letting students correct errors.

Animal	Clothing	Shelter	Transportation
Anaconda	Breeches	Balcony	Dirigible
Armadillo	Chaps	Canopy	Dory
Boar	Jerkin	Colonnade	Gondola
Dromedary	Kilt	Dormer	Icebreaker
Koala	Kimono	Estate	Kayak
Llama	Neckerchief	Hogan	Monorail
Palomino	Obi	Lighthouse	Outrigger
Peccary	Sari	Pagoda	Prairie Schooner*
Tarantula	Sombrero	Silo	Subway*
Zebu	Turban	Veranda	Sulky

Can also be accepted under Shelter

WHAT IS IT?

(A dictionary sheet)

	ANIMAL	CLOTHING	SHELTER	TRANSPORTATION
1.				
2.				
3.				
4.				
5.				
6.				
7.				
8.				
9.				
10.				

Look up each of the words below. Then write it in the correct column.

Anaconda	Estate	Koala	Prairie Schooner
Armadillo	Dory	Lighthouse	Sari
Balcony	Dromedary	Llama	Silo
Boar	Gondola	Monorail	Sombrero
Breeches	Hogan	Neckerchief	Subway
Canopy	Icebreaker	Obi	Sulky
Chaps	Jerkin	Outrigger	Turban
Colonnade	Kayak	Pagoda	Tarantula
Dirigible	Kilt	Palomino	Veranda
Dormer	Kimono	Peccary	Zebu

Weather Wise

Purpose

Follow-up to introductory map lessons

To Make

Enlarge the map and the key so that they are clearly visible to a large group. *(Take them to a copy business to get them blown up larger than a legal size.)* Paste the map and key on a posterboard. Color the water areas on the map blue and the border areas of Canada and Mexico different colors.

Prepare questions that relate to using the key or understanding directions. *(See the sample questions below.)*

To Play

Divide the group into two teams. Ask the first person a question. If the answer is correct, that team gets a point. Continue with the opposing team. Tally the score after all the questions have been answered.

Sample Questions

1. What does the blue area indicate? (*Bodies of water*)

2. What is the difference between the warm and cold keys? (*Triangles pointing opposite directions*)

3. Name one of the bodies of water. (*Pacific Ocean; Atlantic Ocean; Gulf of Mexico; Great Lakes*)

4. Describe the weather in the northwest. (*Rainy*)

5. Where is it warm and sunny? (*Southwest or some Southern states*)

6. Where is your home state? (*Student points*)

7. Where is it windy? (*several answers–Kentucky, Missouri, Hawaii, North Carolina*)

8. What is the weather near the Great Lakes? (*Snowy*)

9. What could be another key for snow?

10. Name one of the larger states and tell what the weather is like.

11. Besides the blue, other areas are shaded a different color. Why? (*Indicates other countries*)

12. Where is Florida located? (*Southeast*)

13. Describe the weather in the central part of the U.S.

14. Describe the weather in Alaska. (*Cold and snowing*)

15. Locate Hawaii.

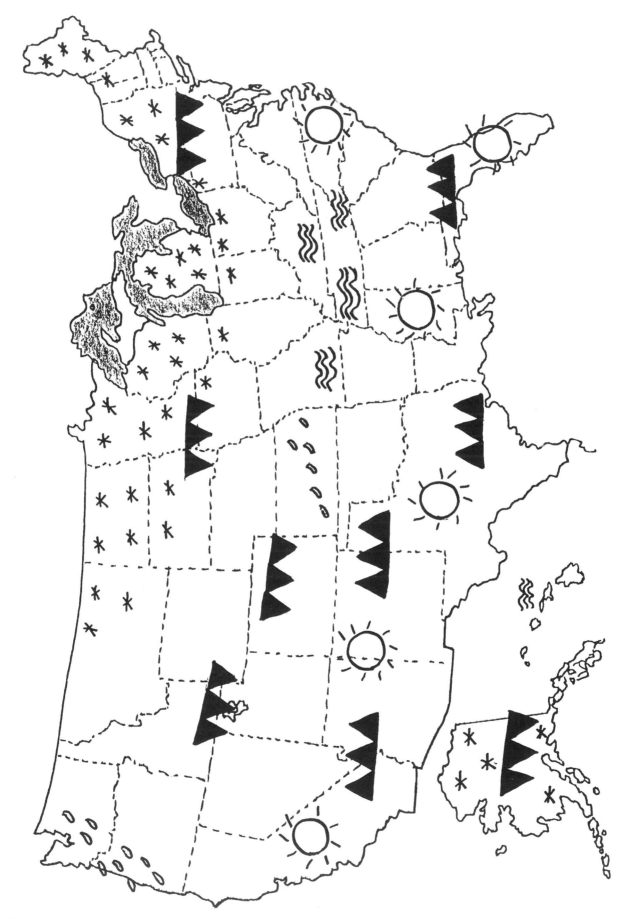

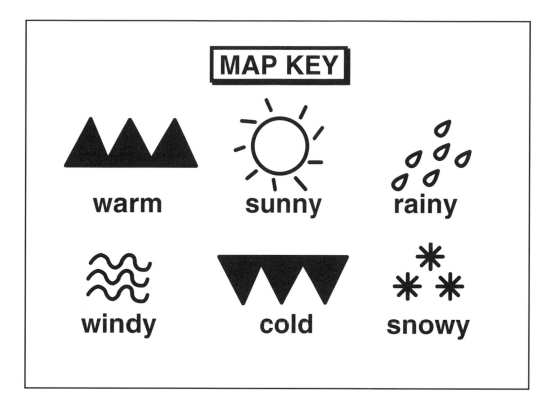

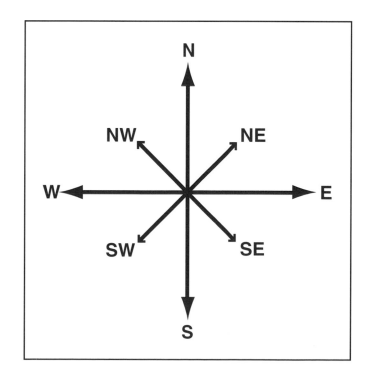

Famous Places

Purpose

An encyclopedia look-it-up activity.

To Make

You need about 30 4X6" cards. (Pastel colors are attractive.)

Find small pictures of famous world places in publishers' catalogs, old geography books, and travel folders. Examples: Mt. Rushmore, Eiffel Tower.

Paste the pictures on one side of the card. Label with the name by which the student is to look up the subject. Example: Great Wall of China.

On the opposite side of the card, type five questions about the subject which can be answered from your reference collection. Prepare an answer sheet for your own checking purposes.

To Use

You might check retention by playing a team game at the next class period. Use some of the questions from the Famous Places cards that are possible for recall. Sample: Name the two falls that constitute Niagara Falls. (American and Horseshoe)

Sample Questions

1. From what kind of stone is the Rock of Gibraltar formed? *(Limestone)*

2. What kind of tower is the Leaning Tower of Pisa? *(Bell tower)*

3. What is the weight of the Liberty Bell? *(2,080 pounds)*

4. How long did it take to sculpt Mt. Rushmore? *(14 years)*

5. What Indian tribe lives in the Grand Canyon? *(Havasupai)*

6. What is beneath the Arch of Triumph? *(Grave of an unknown soldier)*

7. How was the Eiffel Tower used in World War I? *(Observation station)*

8. Where is there another model of the Statue of Liberty? *(Paris)*

9. How many rooms are in the White House? *(132)*

10. In what building is Big Ben? *(House of Parliament)*

11. What do the 36 columns in the Lincoln Memorial stand for? *(Number of states at the time of Lincoln's death)*

Trivia 100

Purpose

Hands-on experience in researching encyclopedias and other reference materials

To Make

Create one hundred questions that can be answered from reference materials in you library: almanac, dictionary, *Guinness*, atlas, electronic encyclopedia, CD-ROM resources, etc. *(See samples on the next pages.)* Using one hundred 3x5" cards, write one question on each card.

Divide the cards into four groups and color code. You can color band the tops of the cards with red, yellow, green, and blue markers or purchase cards in four colors. Number the top corner of each color-banded card (from 1 to 25). Color code four tab cards for organizing the questions.

Prepare two sheets of tablet paper for each table of students in the class. Fold; color band each column; number each column to 25.

To Use

The students at each table work as a team. Each selects a question card, locates the answer in the correct reference tool, and records the answer on the corresponding line of the worksheet (e.g., Red 10, Blue 16).

This activity can be ongoing for as long as four to five weeks. The goal is for each table to answer as many of the one hundred questions as possible.

If you wish to reward good work, you can give small prizes (bookmarks, stickers) to the table members completing the most correct answers. If you want to reward individual effort, have each student initial each answer line contributed to the team worksheet. *(But then, of course, you must tally individual answers!)*

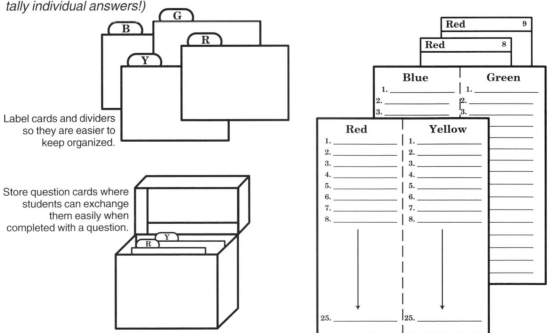

Label cards and dividers so they are easier to keep organized.

Store question cards where students can exchange them easily when completed with a question.

Create answer sheets for each team.

Trivia 100

Red Questions

1. What is the temperature in Mammoth Cave? *(54 degrees F)*

2. Who named the White House? *(Theodore Roosevelt)*

3. What is "hardtack"? *(Ship's biscuit)*

4. What is "Davy Jones' locker"? *(Bottom of the sea)*

5. What is the birthstone for April? *(Diamond)*

6. What two countries border Spain? *(Portugal, France)*

7. What caused the Titanic to sink? *(Iceberg)*

8. How did Mercury serve the Roman gods? *(Messenger)*

9. Where is the tallest waterfall in North America? *(Ribbon Falls, California)*

10. Where is the tallest waterfall in the world? *(Angel Falls, Venezuela)*

11. What is the distance of the Kentucky Derby race? *(1¼ miles)*

12. How old must a horse be to run in the Kentucky Derby? *(3 years)*

13. What four presidents are pictured on Mt. Rushmore?
    (Roosevelt, Lincoln, Jefferson, Washington)

14. What is the highest point in Kentucky? *(Black Mountain)*

15. What is Mauna Loa? *(Volcano)*

16. Where is Mauna Loa? *(Island of Hawaii)*

17. Under what river does the Lincoln Tunnel run? *(Hudson)*

18. Who burned the White House in 1814? *(British)*

19. Where is the Tomb of the Unknown Soldier? *(Arlington, Virginia)*

20. What was Houdini's special kind of magic? *(Escape)*

21. How many floors are in the Empire State Building? *(102)*

22. What is the Taj Mahal made of? *(Marble)*

23. What do BTU's measure? *(Heat)*

24. What is the main food of baleen whales? *(Plankton)*

25. At what rate is the Leaning Tower of Pisa tilting? *(⅟₂₀ of an inch every year)*

Green Questions

1. Who established the Girl Scouts of America? *(Juliette Gordon Law)*

2. What is a poltergeist? *(Noisy ghost)*

3. When was the Great Chicago Fire? *(1871)*

4. According to legend, how did the Chicago fire start?
   (Mrs. O'Leary's cow kicked over a lighted lantern)

5. The Liberty Bell cracked while ringing for a funeral. Whose?
   (Chief Justice John Marshall)

6. Has the Liberty Bell rung since it cracked? *(No, only struck on special occasions)*

7. What is a harmonica? *(Mouth organ)*

8. What are the beginning words to the Gettysburg Address?
   (Four score and seven years ago)

9. Who gave the Gettysburg Address and why?
   (Lincoln was dedicating the Civil War battlefield as a cemetery)

10. What was a "piece of eight"? *(Spanish coin)*

11. In what famous pirate story was the parrot known for calling,
    "Pieces of eight"? *(Treasure Island)*

12. In what mountain range does the Abominable Snowman
    supposedly live? *(Himalayas)*

13. What is the world's largest whale? *(Blue whale)*

14. What was the Hindenburg? *(Airship)*

15. What happened to the Hindenburg? *(Burst into flames while landing)*

16. What do people in Canada call Bigfoot? *(Sasquatch)*

17. How do you enter the Blue Grotto? *(By boat)*

18. What and where is the Blue Grotto? *(Cave on Italian island of Capri)*

19. Name three places to find quicksand. *(Sand bars, bottoms of streams,
    sand flats along seacoasts)*

20. Where did paper get its name? *(Papyrus, a reed used by Egyptians)*

21. What happened to Pompeii? *(Disappeared in volcanic eruption)*

22. Why is Pompeii important today? *(Excavations reveal history)*

23. Where is Alcatraz and when did it close? *(San Francisco Bay, 1963)*

24. What is a won and where is it used? *(Currency of South Korea)*

25. Where and when was did the worst nuclear accident take place? *(1986, Chernobyl)*

Trivia 100

Yellow Questions

1. Who lives in the Vatican Palace? *(The Pope)*

2. What is sauerkraut made of? *(Cabbage)*

3. What was Johnny Appleseed's real name? *(John Chapman)*

4. What team game is rugby very much like? *(Football)*

5. Who invented bifocals? *(Benjamin Franklin)*

6. From what exotic flower does vanilla come? *(Orchid)*

7. What state has been the birthplace of seven presidents? *(Ohio)*

8. How do fish breathe? *(Through gills)*

9. Who is the best-known teller of fables? *(Aesop)*

10. What is the official length of each side of a baseball diamond? *(90 feet)*

11. In what year was Halley's comet scheduled to return? *(2063)*

12. What is quicksilver? *(The metal mercury)*

13. What is the original meaning of penthouse? *(A shed added to a building)*

14. Today, what is a penthouse? *(The top apartment of a tall building)*

15. What should you do with a paw-paw? *(Eat it—it's a fruit)*

16. What fruit does the paw-paw resemble? *(A banana)*

17. Who was the first U.S. Spacewoman? *(Sally Ride)*

18. In the Greek alphabet, what does "Ω" represent? *(W)*

19. Find a table of Weights and Measures. What is a dozen dozen? *(Gross)*

20. How many dry quarts are in a bushel? *(32)*

21. What is the real name of Dr. Seuss? *(Theodor Seuss Geisel)*

22. Where was Thomas A. Becket murdered? *(Canterbury Cathedral)*

23. Why was Becket murdered? *(The king's knights thought the king desired Becket's death)*

24. What was the date of Thomas Becket's murder? *(December 29, 1170)*

25. What remained in Pandora's box when she shut the lid? *(Hope)*

Blue Questions

1. Who was the youngest U.S. president to be inaugurated? *(Theodore Roosevelt)*

2. How old was the youngest U.S. president at the time of his inauguration? *(42 years old)*

3. How many days does it take a chicken egg to hatch? *(21)*

4. What do the four "Hs" stand for in 4H? *(Head, heart, hands, health)*

5. How long did Rip VanWinkle sleep? *(20 years)*

6. What is the common name for sodium chloride? *(Salt)*

7. Why was Benjamin Franklin's portrait chosen for one of the first U.S. postage stamps? *(He was the first U.S. postmaster)*

8. Who in addition to Ben Franklin was portrayed on early U.S. postage stamps? *(George Washington)*

9. Easter dates vary. In the year 2000, what day will Easter occur? *(April 23)*

10. Between what two dates must Easter Fall? *(March 22 and April 25)*

11. Why was Frederick Chopin famous? *(Composer)*

12. What was the name of the first comic strip? *(Hogan's Alley)*

13. In what year did the first comic strip appear? *(1893)*

14. In what year was the first Christmas card used? *(1851)*

15. What was the size of the largest popsicle? *(5,750 pounds)*

16. What was the size of the largest bubble gum bubble? *(22 inches)*

17. What are the largest trees in the world? *(Sequoia)*

18. What country is divided into the North Island and the South Island? *(New Zealand)*

19. Name three of the seven Hawaiian Islands. *(Hawaii, Oahu, Molokai, Maui, Lanai, Kauai, Niihau)*

20. Where is the aurora borealis seen? *(Northern Hemisphere sky)*

21. What Vice President was tried for treason? *(Aaron Burr)*

22. What are the first seven words of the U.S. Constitution? *(We, the people of the United States)*

23. Where should you go to get a good view of the Aurora Borealis? *(20 degrees from the magnetic poles)*

24. Which U.S. state has the lowest population? *(Wyoming)*

25. Who is Babe Didrickson Zaharias? *(Greatest U.S. woman athlete)*

Who Am I?

Purpose

To review biography books

To Make

Duplicate brief descriptions of at least twenty famous people for all students. *(See examples on the following pages.)* Write their names on small cards, one name per card. Put the cards in a paper grocery bag.

You will need a timer.

To Play

Divide the group into two teams. Set the timer for two minutes. Adjust the time limit as you determine necessary. The first player picks a card out of the paper bag. The opposing team members ask questions about the person whose name is on the card. The player answers the questions according to the information given on the sheets. When the time is up, the team by consensus decides on the mystery person. If correct that team gets a point.

Continue with the other team. Continue with alternate turns until the cards are all gone or the class time is over.

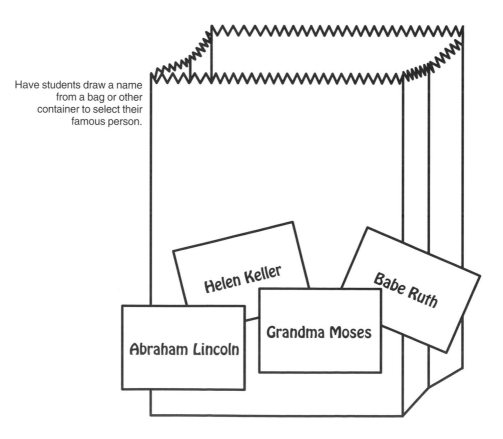

Have students draw a name from a bag or other container to select their famous person.

Who Am I? Examples

Marian Anderson

I was born to poor parents. I became the first African American to sing with the Metropolitan Opera Company. I received the Presidential Medal of Freedom.

Clara Barton

I was called the "Angel of the Battlefield." I carried supplies and nursed the soldiers during the Civil War. I founded the American Red Cross.

Alexander Graham Bell

I taught the deaf. I was a scientist. I invented the telephone.

George Washington Carver

I was born a slave. I became a college professor. I developed products for sweet potatoes, pecans, and over 300 products for peanuts.

Benjamin Franklin

I invented the bifocals and the Franklin stove. I showed the world that lightning is electricity. I was the only one to sign all four important documents in our history—the Declaration of Independence, the Constitution, the Treaty of Paris, and the Treaty of Alliance with France.

Helen Keller

I was unable to see or hear. I learned to speak and read with Braille. I graduated from college and wrote many books.

Martin Luther King, Jr.

I was a minister. I led the peaceful protest to gain equal rights for African Americans. I received the Novel peace prize and am honored with a national holiday.

Abraham Lincoln

I was born in a log cabin in Kentucky. I became the 16th president of the U.S. The Civil Was was fought during my term as president. Many slaves were freed because of me.

Grandma Moses

I started painting when I was 76 years old. I painted 25 pictures after my 100th birthday. I painted scenes of rural life I remembered from my childhood.

Paul Revere

I was a silversmith who made that famous ride to warn the colonists that the British soldiers were coming. I later made the copper fittings for the ship "Old Ironsides."

Who Am I?

Franklin Delano Roosevelt

I was the only president to be elected four times. I served as president for twelve years. I saw my country through the Great Depression and World War II.

Betsy Ross

I was visited by Gen . George Washington. He asked me to make a flag with starts and stripes, said to be the first American flag that had them. The flag was officially adopted on June 14, 1777.

Babe Ruth

I set a record of 714 regular season home runs. In one season I made 60 home runs. I was named to the National Baseball Hall of Fame.

Sacagawea

I was born Shoshoni Indian. My name means "Bird Woman." I was a guide for the Lewis and Clark expedition.

Sequoyah

I was a Cherokee Indian. I invented a system of writing for the Cherokees. Many learned to read and write as a result. Books and newspapers were published in our language.

Squanto

I was a Patuxet Indian. I showed the Pilgrims how to plant corn and to fish. Many at Plymouth Colony survived with my help.

Harriet Tubman

I was born a slave. I guided more than 300 slaves to freedom. I used the Underground Railroad.

Mark Twain

My real name is Samuel Clemens. I wrote *The Adventures of Huckleberry Finn* and *The Adventures of Tom Sawyer.* I gathered stories as I traveled around the world.

George Washington

I led our soldiers during the Revolutionary War. I was our first president. My home is at Mt. Vernon.

Biography Bingo

Purpose

To encourage reading of biography and to introduce some famous personages to the students

To Make

Each student will need a 9"-square Bingo card. Grid the card in 3" squares. In each square, put names and/or pictures of notable people, preferably those for whom you have biography titles. You can use publishers' catalogs or discarded magazines for pictures of personalities. No two boards should be exactly alike or the students will Bingo together. You will need at least 30 names to create 30 interesting bingo cards.

Get together enough markers (cardboard discs, plastic chips, dry beans) to cover all the squares in case you play a cover-all.

Print a strip (10x2") with each name from the game. When called, place each in a sentence tray so the class can see it.

To Play

Distribute Bingo cards and markers. Bingo can be played several ways: three in a row, four corners, postage stamp (four adjoining squares) or cover all. Several games can be played in a class period. You might want to award simple prizes such as bookmarks or stickers.

Option: To promote facts about these famous persons, ask questions occasionally and give a special marker to the student answering correctly, that marker to be used on any square needed by the player to win.

Samples: Name a book written by Mark Twain.

During what war did Lincoln serve as President?

Mark Twain	Hillary Clinton	Abraham Lincoln
Christa McAuliffe	George Washington	Whitney Houston
Michael Jordan	Kristi Yamaguchi	Henry Ford

I ❤ Books

Purpose

To review skills related to various kinds of books or to promote student interest in books. Difficulty of the questions will determine grade level.

To Make

You will need a pocket chart or you will need to make a board with slots. On a tagboard strip, write **I ❤ BOOKS**.

Cut approximately 25 Valentine hearts out of construction paper. On the hearts, write:

        5 points *(write on 7 hearts)*

        10 points *(write on 6 hearts)*

        15 points *(write on 5 hearts)*

        20 points *(write on 4 hearts)*

        25 points *(write on 3 hearts)*

        TREAT *(optional) (write on 1 heart)*

Place hearts in the slots with point values hidden from view.

To Play

Divide the class into two teams. Alternate asking questions. If a team member answers a question correctly, let that person pick a heart to determine the number of points earned for that answer. If it is a Treat card, give a bookmark or a paperback book but no points. The side with the most points wins.

Game board

General Fiction Questions for I ♥ Books

1. Where is the fiction section?
2. How do you recognize a fiction call number? *(No numbers; three letters)*
3. What do the three letters of a fiction call number stand for? *(First three letters of author's last name)*
4. In what type of order are fiction books shelved? *(Alphabetical)*
5. How are fiction call numbers different from nonfiction call numbers? *(Fiction call numbers do not have numbers)*
6. Tell me the title of a fiction book.
7. Tell me the author of a fiction book.
8. What does fiction mean? *(Not true)*
9. Tell me the call number for a fiction book by C.S. Lewis. *(LEW)*
10. Where in the fiction section will a book by C.S. Lewis be, beginning, middle or end? *(Middle)*
11. Find a book by Patricia McKissack on the shelf.
12. Which of these fiction books would come first on the shelf?
    All About Sam by Lois Lowry   or   *The Wish Giver* by Bill Brittain   *(The Wish Giver)*
13. Put this fiction book (hand to student) back on the shelf.
14. Would *The Guinness Book of World Records* be found in the fiction section? *(No)*
15. Would *Bunnicula* be found in the fiction section? *(Yes)*
16. Would a book about Christopher Columbus be found in the fiction section? *(No)*
17. Are biography call numbers and fiction call numbers formed the same way? *(No)*
18. Are fiction call numbers and easy fiction formed the same way? *(Yes)*
19. Which of these fiction call numbers comes last? MOO, MIL, MAC   *(MOO)*
20. Would folktales be found in the fiction section? *(No)*

Story and Character Fiction Questions for I ♥ Books

1. Where did Mrs. Frisby's rat friend escape from? (NIMH, *Mrs. Frisby and the Rats of NIMH*)
2. Describe the fabulous furnace of the Finches. (A volcano, *Finches' Fabulous Furnace*)
3. What was the owl planning to eat on his Tuesday birthday? (A toad, *A Toad for Tuesday*)
4. Where did Brighty the Mule live? (Grand Canyon, *Brights of Grand Canyon*)
5. Where did Omri put the plastic Indian he got for his birthday? (In the cupboard)
6. What recipe uses grape juice, vinegar, olive oil, mustard, mayonnaise, etc.? (Freckle Juice)
7. Who am I describing? She was nine years old, orphaned, and a sight in mismatched socks and patched clothes. (Pippi Longstocking)
8. In what book does Aslan the lion battle the witch of Narnia? *(The Lion, the Witch, and the Wardrobe)*
9. Who is "fantastic" as he outwits the farmers Boggis, Bunce, and Bean? (Fantastic Mr. Fox)
10. Who did Amos help to write the Declaration of Independence? (Benjamin Franklin, *Ben and Me*)
11. Who were the "most horrible kids in the history of the world" who took part in a Christmas pageant? (The Herdsman, *Best Christmas Pageant Ever*)
12. What were the hundred dresses made of? (Paper, *Hundred Dresses*)
13. What is the name of Henry Higgin's dog? (Ribsy)
14. Who said? "I will come by train. I will wear a yellow bonnet. I am plain and tall." (Sarah)
15. Who was Charlotte's friend in *Charlotte's Web*? (Wilbur)

Caldecott Matches

Purpose

To review Caldecott Medal winners

To Make

Cut fourteen book pockets down to 2" high. Paste the pockets in two columns on a posterboard, seven in each column, as shown below. Cut seven pieces of yarn about 42" long. (Using different colors of yarn makes this game more colorful.) Double each piece of yarn and put a twist tie at the center point to make a threading point.

Make a small hole next to each pocket with a hammer and small nail. Then taking the yarn pieces, attach one yarn piece to each of the holes in the left-hand column. This is done by threading the twist-tie end through the posterboard from the back and knotting the loose ends of yarn on the backside of the board. Leave the twist-tie end hanging loose.

Write titles of Caldecott Medal winners on cards that fit into the pockets. You may decorate some with pictures from book club flyers or publishers' catalogs. Write words from objects that are related to the stories. Make at least fourteen matches (two rounds).

Examples: *Lon PoPo* (wolf); *Jumanji* (volcano); *Funny Little Woman* (rice paddle); *Mirette on the High Wire* (top hat); *Make Way for Ducklings* (policeman); *Tuesday* (frog); *Polar Express* (train); *Why Mosquitoes Buzz in People's Ears* (monkey); *One Fine Day* (fox); *Snowy Day* (stick); *Biggest Bear* (maple sugar).

To Play

Place the cards in the pockets, titles on one side and matches on the other. Divide the group into two teams. Ask the first player to make a match. If correct, thread the yarn from the title to the word and give that team a point. If incorrect, leave the match for another player to answer. Continue by alternating teams. After all matches have been made, remove the cards and put another set on the board. Unthread the yarn. Keep a tally of points from each round and declare the winner after several rounds.

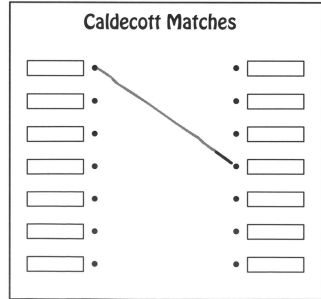

Game board

Go Caldecott

Purpose

To review Caldecott Medal winners

To Make

Cut out pictures of Caldecott Medal winners from a Caldecott Medal poster. (Perma-Bound Books has posters). Paste around the edge of a large posterboard. If you are unable to get a poster, write titles and their illustrators instead. Designate a spot for GO and two spots for Opportunity.

Use the samples for Opportunity cards to make at least eight cards. Prepare Caldecott questions. *(See examples for opportunity cards and questions on the next page.)*

You will need a dice or spinner and clothespins or clamps.

To Play

Divide the group into two teams. Ask the first person a Caldecott question. If the player gives a correct answer, that person throws the dice or spins the spinner to determine the number of moves to make. Use the clothespin or clamp to serve as a marker. If the marker rests on an Opportunity spot, read from one of the Opportunity cards. Move the marker to the title that is mentioned on the card. Continue the same procedure with a player from the opposing team. Each time the marker passes GO, the team receives 1 point. Play until the end of a designated time period. The team with the most points is declared the winner.

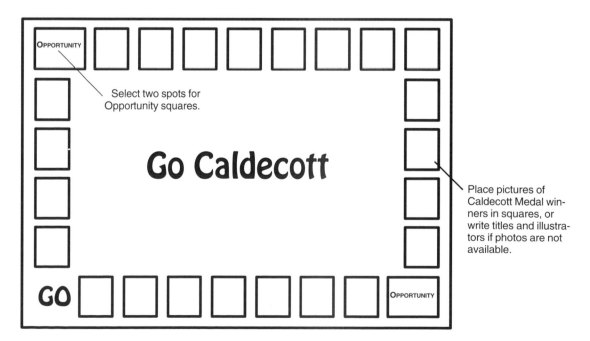

Sample Opportunity Cards

1. Sail to *Where the Wild Things Are*. If you pass Go, collect 1 point.

2. Hurry to join the search for *Sylvester*. Do not stop to collect 1 point at Go.

3. Listen to the *Sky God* tell a story. Pay the price of 1 point.

4. Take a walk to enjoy the beauty of *Owl Moon*. If you pass Go collect 2 pts.

5. Pay to see *Mirette On the High Wire*. But collect 1 point if you pass Go.

6. Fly on a lily pad on *Tuesday*. Slow down to collect 1 point at Go.

7. Board the *Polar Express* for an exciting trip. Collect 3 points for a gift.

8. The *Funny Little Woman* is chasing her rice dumpling. Help her catch it. The magic puddle helps double 1 point if you pass Go.

Caldecott Medal Sample Questions

1. Who receives the Caldecott Medal? *(The illustrator)*

2. How many illustrators win the Caldecott Medal each year? *(Only one)*

3. Where can you find information on the illustrator and the publisher? *(Title page)*

4. Which one of these books has a kingdom as its setting? *Sylvester and the Magic Pebble; Biggest Bear; Many Moons* *(Many Moons)*

5. Is *Tuesday* a fiction or nonfiction book? *(Fiction)*

6. Do Caldecott Medal books have indexes? *(No)*

7. Do most Caldecott Medal books have a table of contents? *(No)*

8. Where is the call number on the book? *(Spine)*

9. A wild rumpus occurs in what story? *(Where the Wild Things Are)*

10. What is *Jumanji*? *(Board game)*

11. Which story has an orchard as part of the setting? *(The Biggest Bear)*

12. What did the fox lose in *One Fine Day*? *(His tail)*

13. Which book has donkeys and pigs as characters? *(Sylvester and the Magic Pebble)*

14. What character enjoyed a lump of maple sugar? *(The Biggest Bear)*

15. Where did the grandfather visit in Grandfather's Journey? *(America)*

16. What fairy tale is *Lon Po Po* similar to? *("Red Riding Hood")*

17. What character feels guilty for all the troubles in *Why Mosquitoes Buzz in People's Ears*. *(The mosquito)*

18. What did Peter lose at the end of the *Snowy Day*? *(His snowball)*

19. What book is made up of short stories with animal characters and plots that teach lessons. *(Fables)*

20. What did the *Funny Little Woman* use the magic paddle for? *(To cook rice)*

21. What was shaped like a star in *Nine Days to Christmas*? *(A piñata)*

Go Newbery

Purpose

To review Newbery Medal winners.

To Make

Follow directions for Go Caldecott but use Newbery Medal pictures or titles instead. Some samples for Opportunity cards are listed below.

To Play

Use the directions for Go Caldecott.

Sample Newbery Medal Opportunity Cards

1. *The Whipping Boy* is on the run. Share a day of adventures with him. Collect 1 point if you pass Go.

2. Journey to the plains with Sarah. If you pass Go, collect 1 point.

3. Sail to the *Island of the Blue Dolphins*. Collect 1 point if you pass Go.

4. You inherit 2 points. Hurry to the *Westing Game* to collect.

5. Ride the *King of the Wind*. Collect 2 points as you fly by Go.

6. Sell the maple syrup collected from Maple Hill. Charge 3 points for it.

7. Pass through *A Wrinkle in Time* and double all the points that you have earned.

8. Mrs. Frisby is in distress. Go to see how you can be of help. Collect 2 points if you pass Go.

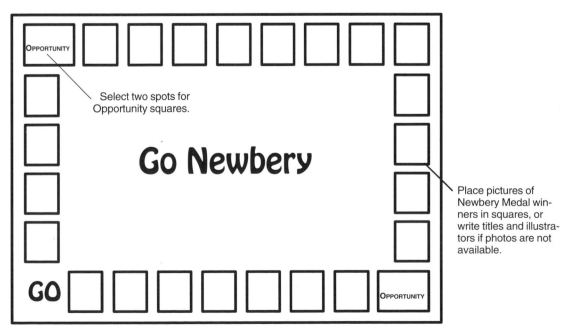

OPPORTUNITY

Select two spots for Opportunity squares.

Go Newbery

Place pictures of Newbery Medal winners in squares, or write titles and illustrators if photos are not available.

GO

OPPORTUNITY

Newbery Medal Questions

1. Is the Newbery Medal given to the author or illustrator.   *(Author)*

2. Are all Newbery Medal award winners fiction? *(No)*

3. What kind of book is *Lincoln*?   *(A biography)*

4. Is *Joyful Noise: Poems for Two Voices* fiction or nonfiction? *(Nonfiction)*

5. What is the call number for *The Giver,* written by Lois Lowry? *(F Low)*

6. Is *The High King*, written by Lloyd Alexander, at the beginning, middle, or end of the fiction section?   *(Beginning)*

7. What is the call number for *Lincoln: A Photobiography*?   *(B Lin)*

8. What animal appears as one of the main characters in both *Sounder* and *Shiloh*? *(A dog)*

9. True or False? An author is not permitted to receive a second Newbery Medal if he or she has previously won one. *(False)*

10. True or False? The call number of a fiction Newbery Medal book comes from the title of the book. *(False)*

11. What character is punished for the bad behavior of another person? *(The Whipping Boy)*

12. *Johnny Tremain* was set during what historical period in our country? *(Revolutionary War)*

13. Give the title of a Newbery Medal winner that is set in another country.   *(Number the Stars, The Giver, etc.)*

14. In what book were the characters used as experimental animals?   *(Mrs. Frisby and the Rats of NIMH)*

15. True or False? Shiloh takes place during the Civil War.   *(False)*

16. Who wrote *Dear Mr. Henshaw*? *(Beverly Cleary)*

17. A death occurs in several Newbery Medal books. Name one. *(Bridge to Terabithea; Missing May)*

18. A character searches for her father in what Newbery Medal book? *(A Wrinkle in Time)*

19. True or False? *The Giver* is best described as historical fiction? *(False)*

20. True or False? Lois Lowry won two Newbery Medal awards— for *Number the Stars* and *The Giver.* *(True)*

21. Name one Newbery Medal winner that has African American characters. *(Roll of Thunder; Hear My Cry; M.C. Higgins; Maniac Magee, etc.)*

Magic Hat

Purpose

To focus on the folk and fairy tale section of the media center.

To Make

Paste a picture of a magician's hat on the side of a large grocery bag. Put the call number for the folk and fairy tale books, 398.2, on the hat.

Write questions *(See sample list.)* related to these books on cards. Put the cards in the bag.

To Play

Divide the class into two teams. Direct the first player to pull a question card from the bag and answer the question. If correct the team gets a point. If incorrect put the question back into the bag. Continue the same procedure with the other team. When all the questions have been answered, tally the score and declare the winner.

Paste top hat pattern on a grocery bag to create you Magic Hat Bag.

Sample Questions: Folk and Fairy Tales

1. The Chinese tale of Lon Po Po and the tale of Little Red Riding Hood have a similar character. Who character is it? *(A wolf)*

2. Which characters' father was a poor woodcutter? *(Hansel and Gretel; Momotaro)*

3. What did Jack swap for the magic beans? *(A cow)*

4. Who lived in a hut that stood on chicken feet? *(Baba Yaga)*

5. Who did not have a good night's sleep despite sleeping on 20 mattresses and 20 featherbeds? *(Princess and the Pea)*

6. Where did Rapunzel's name come from? *(Salad greens)*

7. An acorn fell on what character's head causing her to panic? *(Henny Penny)*

8. What story has a coachman, footmen, and stepsisters? *(Cinderella)*

9. Describe two of the Bremen Town musicians. *(Donkey, dog, cat, rooster)*

10. Whose name meant "the most wonder thing in the whole wide world?" *(Tikki Tikki Tembo)*

11. Who stuck two sticks in his ears to keep from hearing nonsense? *(Iguana in Why Mosquitoes Buzz in People's Ears)*

12. What Greek slave collected short stories that teach a moral or give good advice? *(Aesop)*

13. What is the family name of two German brothers who collected fairy tales? *(Grimm)*

14. Who wrote such stories as *The Ugly Duckling* and *The Emperor's New Clothes*? *(Hans Christian Andersen)*

15. What did an old Japanese woman find in a peach floating down the river? *(A baby – Momotaro)*

16. What spider character is popular in African folktales? *(Anansi)*

17. What are Indian paintbrushes? *(Flowers)*

18. What did the six foolish fishermen forget to do? *(Each forgot to count himself)*

19. What tool did John Henry use in his race against the steam drill? *(Hammer)*

20. What did Rumpelstiltskin do to help the miller's daughter? *(Spin straw into gold)*

21. Finish the sentence: "I'll run and run as fast as I can. You can't catch me. I'm the _____!" *(Gingerbread Man)*

22. How many blackbirds were baked in a pie to serve before the king? *(24)*

23. What was the "sacred dog" the people received from the Great Spirit in *The Gift of the Sacred Dog*? *(Horse)*

24. Who had an ox named Babe? *(Paul Bunyan)*

25. What did the Sky God give to Anansi for bringing him the leopard of-the-terrible-teeth, the hornet who-stings-like-fire, and the fairy whom-men-never-see? *(Stories)*

Name That Book!

Purpose

To promote fiction books.

To Make

Mount six fiction book jackets on posterboard and laminate. Cut them out as puzzles. Put the pieces of each book jacket in a sandwich bag (six sandwich bags in all).

You will need a large paper grocery bag or other container from which students can pull the puzzle pieces.

Prepare a list of questions or use some of the sample questions for general board games at the end of this book.

To Play

Divide the group into two teams. Put one puzzle in the large paper grocery bag. Ask the first player a question. If the response is correct, the player pulls a puzzle piece from the bag and lays it on a table. Continue with a player from the other team. If the answer is incorrect that player does not get to take a puzzle piece. The players may begin to fit the puzzle together at any time.

After each correct response, a player may state the title of the mystery book. If the player correctly identifies the title, that team wins the match. If incorrect the opposing team is declared the winner by default. The title is announced. Continue playing other rounds as time permits. After each round remove the remaining puzzle pieces from the bag.

Mount the book jacket on posterboard, laminate and then cut into puzzle pieces.

Twelve Questions

Purpose

To familiarize students with particular fiction titles and to promote creative thinking.

To Make

Cut a large circle out of posterboard or use a large pizza board. Write the numbers 1 to 12 around the edge of the board. Beside these numbers put point values to be earned. *(See drawing on the next page.)*

You will also need a clothespin, large paper clip or clamp to serve as a marker.

Create a list of titles from your collection that you would like to introduce to your students. You may duplicate this list as a handout or write the titles on the chalkboard. You will also need to write the titles on 3x5" cards, one per card.

To Play

Hand out the list of titles to students or write them on the board. Place the stack of title cards on a table and draw one to begin the game. Explain that each team will be allowed to ask twelve "yes" or "no" questions in order to identify the name of the book on the card you are holding. That regardless of the answer to a particular question, you will move the clip one space for each question asked. The team may stop at any point to identify the title. If the answer is wrong, the team receives no points for that round. If correct, they receive the number of points shown on the board. Continue by drawing another title card and directing the second team to follow the same procedure. Add up the scores at the end of the game. The team with the most points wins.

Sample Questions

1. Is there a name of an animal in the title?
2. Are there more than two words in the title?
3. Is there a person's name in the title?
4. Is there a number in the title?
5. Does the title have the words an, and, or the?
6. Does the title have a Mr. or Mrs.?
7. Does the title indicate a geographic area?
8. Is there a name of a color in the title?
9. Are there more than four words in the title?
10. Does the title begin with the letters R to Z?
11. Does the title have the word of in it?
12. Does the title have a day of the week, a month, or the name of a season?

Twelve Questions

Alphabet Soup

Purpose

A "quickie" activity that reviews titles, authors, and subjects

Example:

EN _ _ _ _ O _ E _ IA   _ _ O _ N   _ E _ S   _ IS   _ AN

(Encyclopedia Brown Gets His Man)

To Play

Select a title, subject, or author name. On a chalkboard, indicate the number of letters in the words with dashes. Let students take turns suggesting letters that might be in the answer, which are then written in. See who can guess!

Option: In lieu of a chalkboard, make alphabet cards that can be displayed in a sentence chart. You will need multiples of the vowels and most-used consonants. Leave at least an inch on the bottom edge of each card where it will insert into the card tray.

Alphabet cards should have at least an inch of space at the bottom to allow cards to fit securely in the card tray.

Think Tac Toe

Purpose

To promote creative thinking.

To Make

Cut nine 8½x11" cards and paste an X and an O on each card, one on each side so that cards can be flipped up to show either an X or an O.

Prepare a set of questions for the game. *(See example on p. 122)*

To Play

Select nine students to be panel members and two students to be contestants.
Direct them to sit:

	Student Panel		
Three on a table	X	X	X
Three on a chair	X	X	X
Three on the floor	X	X	X
Facing the panel:	C	T	C
Teacher (T)			
Contestants (C)			

Have the panel face towards the class and have the contestants face towards the panel. Give each panel member a card that has the O and X on it, and direct them to leave the cards in their laps. Designate the X to one contestant and the O to the other.

The starting player begins by picking a panel member to answer the first question. The teacher gives the question and the panel member answers. The contestant decides to agree or disagree with the answer.

If the response is correct

If the answer is correct and the contestant agrees, he earns a mark.

If the answer is correct and the contestant disagrees, he earns no mark.

If the response is incorrect

If the answer is incorrect and the contestant agrees, he earns no mark.

If the answer is incorrect and the contestant disagrees, he earns a mark.

Alternate questions until there is a tic-tac-toe or three marks in a row. Change contestants.

Think Tac Toe Sample Questions

1. What country is said to be the home of the Loch Ness monster?

   a) England   b) Ireland   c) Scotland   *(C)*

2. Footprints as large as a size 14 shoe have been sighted in the Northwest. What creature is said to have made those footprints?   *(Bigfoot)*

3. The Abominable Snowman names Yeti lives in the Himalayas. Which country does not have parts of the Himalayan mountains?

   a) Tibet   b) Japan   c) Nepal   *(B)*

4. Stories of trolls were found in Scandinavian folk tales. Name a Scandinavian country. *(Denmark, Norway, or Sweden)*

5. What wrinkled little men were sought after in Ireland because they boasted of hidden pots of gold?   *(Leprechauns*

6. Stories of these ugly and mischievous people who liked to pinch and beat naughty children and sour milk were told in France. Who were they?   *(Goblins)*

7. What noisy ghosts would sometimes break dishes and make pictures fall? They were the residents of haunted houses?   *(Poltergeists)*

8. What does UFO stand for?

   a) Unidentified flying object   b) Unusually fast object   c) Unknown foreign object *(A)*

9. Who scooped out the Great Lakes to get drinking water for his pet ox? *(Paul Bunyan)*

10. Who rode on a cyclone and dug out the Rio Grande River? *(Pecos Bill)*

11. Who used two hand-held hammers to win a drilling contest against a steam drill? *(John Henry)*

12. How many years did Rip Van Winkle sleep? *(20)*

13. Where did Liliuokalani rule as the last queen? She wrote "Aloha Oe." *(Hawaii)*

14. What winged horse can sometimes be seen in the evening sky? *(Pegasus)*

15. Who created the character called "the Grinch"?   *(Dr. Seuss)*

16. Who was once reported to have killed 105 bears in nine months?

    a) Daniel Boone b) Davy Crockett   c) Annie Oakley   *(B)*

17. Who was the famous resident of Sleepy Hollow? *(Ichabod Crane)*

18. Who placed her head on his and thereby saved Captain John Smith's life? *(Pocahontas)*

19. What Greek slave made popular short stories of animals that ended with lessons in good or foolish behavior? *(Aesop)*

20. What is the family name of the two German brothers who collected German fairy tales? *(Grimm)*

21. King Midas laughed and cried when everything he touched turned to _____. *(Gold)*

22. Who told the tale of the Ugly Duckling?   *(Hans Christian Andersen)*

23. Where did the Anansi stories come from?   *(Africa)*

City Tour

Purpose

An enrichment activity to follow-up a unit on the community or city.

To Make

Paste about twelve pockets on a posterboard. Write the names of places in the community on these pockets. Decorate the pockets with pictures cut from brochures.

Cut twelve slips of one color and twelve slips of another color out of construction paper. Write: **ADMISSION TICKET** on each slip of paper.

Write at least three questions on twelve 3x5" index cards and put these cards in the pockets on the posterboard.

To Play

Divide the class into two teams. Give each team twelve admission tickets. Explain that to win the team must be the first to successfully visit all the city sights and give up all twelve tickets.

Direct the first player to pick a city sight. Read a question from that pocket. If that player gives the correct answer, take a ticket and put it in the pocket. Continue the game with the second team following the same procedure. The player does not have to pick the same sight, but can do so. No player may pick a city sight already successfully visited by his team. If a player responds incorrectly, do not accept an ADMISSION TICKET. That team must revisit that sight sometime again. The first team to give up all tickets wins the game.

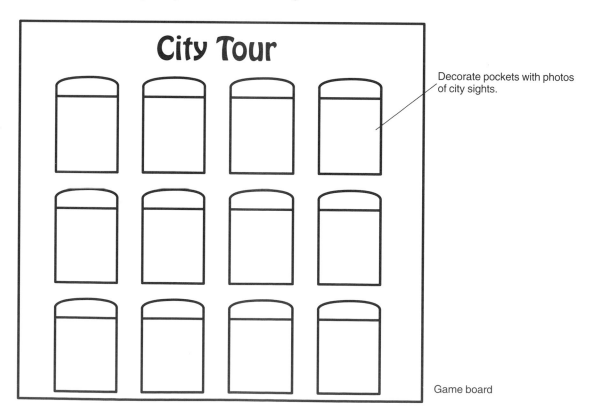

Decorate pockets with photos of city sights.

Game board

City Tour Sample Questions

Airport

1. What direction is the airport from your home?

2. What is the name of the airport?

3. What major highway is close to the airport?

Museum

1. Which of these would be most helpful in finding out when the museum opens on Saturday:

   a. dictionary
   b. newspaper
   c. telephone book

2. Which of these would most likely not be seen at a museum?

   a. seesaw
   b. sculpture
   c. mural

3. A curator works at a museum. What can help you find out what a curator does?

   a. an atlas
   b. a dictionary
   c. a globe

Hospital

1. Which of these does not work in a hospital?

   a. surgeon
   b. athlete
   c. dietician

2. If you have to stay in a hospital, are you an outpatient?

3. Which hospital is closest to your home?

Game Cubes

Cubes are needed for several of the games in this book. On the next page is a pattern you can reproduce to make your own cubes.

You can also make specialty cubes that can be used for games all by themselves. Here are some examples:

Paste miniature pictures of books from book club catalogs on all sides of three cubes. Direct players to toss the three cubes and to alphabetize the titles or authors of the books facing up.

Write call numbers on all sides of three cubes. Direct players to toss the three cubes and to put the call numbers that are facing up in the correct order.

Write one letter of the alphabet on each side of the three cubes. Do not repeat a letter. Direct a player to toss the three cubes and to pick one of the three letters that is facing up. The player must come up with a title of a book that begins with that letter. Tell students that A, An, and The at the beginning of a title are omitted.

2-Inch Cube Pattern

1. Fold on dotted lines.

2. Paste together at the tabs.

3. Stuff the cube with newspaper to give body to the cube.

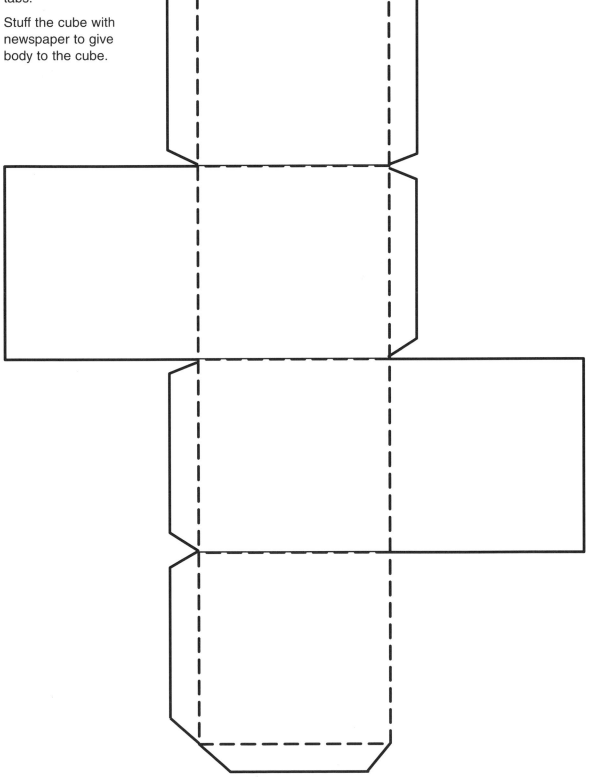

Number Patterns

Either cut out or reproduce these two number pages to make the Memory and Media Manners games.

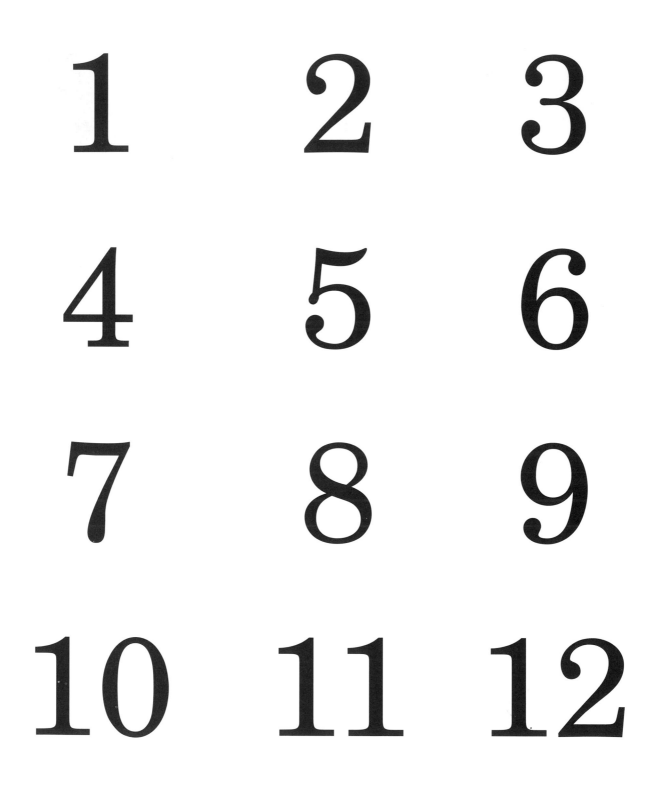

13 14 15

16 17 18

19 20

Easel Pattern

Cut from cardboard or even wood. Light cardboard will fold but heavy-weight will lend better support if you cut two separate pieces, tape well down the center, then fold. You would hinge the wooden pieces.

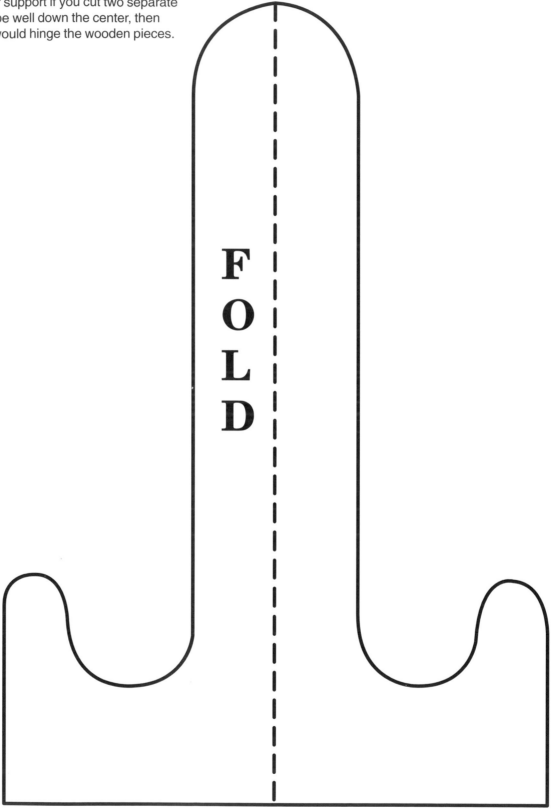

**F
O
L
D**

130

Sample Questions for General Board Games

1. What does an author do? *(Writes books)*

2. What does an illustrator do? *(Draws pictures)*

3. What does a publisher do? *(Prints books)*

4. What do you call the name of any book? *(Title)*

5. How does a copyright protect an author? *(No one has the right to copy without the author's permission)*

6. Describe the copyright symbol. *(C in a circle)*

7. What information follows the copyright symbol? *(Year the book was published)*

8. On what page do you find the publishing information? *(Title page)*

9. Is the publishing information generally found at the top, middle, or bottom of the title page? *(Bottom)*

10. Name the six items of information you might find on the title page. *(Author, title, illustrator, publisher, copyright, city, date)*

11. What part of a book will you find the title page and contents? *(Front part of a book)*

12. The following words are clues to what information: written by , story by, by? *(Author)*

13. The following words are clues to what information on the title page: with drawings by, pictures by, illustrated by? *(Illustrator)*

14. Which page comes first, the title page or the contents page? *(Title page)*

15. Where does the copyright date appear on the title page? *(Bottom front page or verso of title page)*

16. What helps sometimes appear at the end of a book? *(Index, bibliography, glossary)*

17. Where do you find the call numbers on a book? *(Spine)*

18. What other information may be on the spine of a book? *(Author, title, publisher)*

19. What does fiction mean? *(Not true)*

20. Name a fiction author.

21. Tell a title by that author.

22. What would be the call number for that book?

23. Where is our online catalog?

24. What is its purpose? *(A list of the library holdings)*

25. How is it arranged? *(Alphabetical by author, title,subject, can be sorted in many ways)*

26. Name three kinds of records in the catalog. *(Author,title, subject)*

27. What three words do you omit as the first word of a title? *(A, an, the)*

Sample Questions

28. True or False? Most of the information in the computer catalog comes from the title page of a book. *(True)*

29. Which is the subject, A or B? A. True Book of Insects, B. INSECTS. *(B)*

30. Which one tells the number of pages, A or B? A. 629.1 B. 69 p. *(B)*

31. What do you call true books? *(Nonfiction)*

32. What is used for the call numbers of nonfiction? *(Numbers)*

33. How do these numbers help us? *(To find books by subject matter)*

34. Who devised this classification system? *(Melvil Dewey)*

35. Nonfiction books are divided into how many major classes? *(Ten)*

36. Which one of these would tend to be nonfiction—science fiction, reference or story collection? *(Reference)*

37. What do you call a book about a person who really lived? *(Biography)*

38. In our library, what is the call number for biography? *(B)*

39. Where do we get the letters for the second line of a nonfiction call number? *(First three letters, last name of author)*

40. Where do we get the letters for the second line of a biography call number? *(First two letters, last name of person the book is about)*

41. Where do we get the letters for a fiction call number? *(First three letters, last name of author)*

42. Name a person we might have a biography about.

43. Print that call number on the chalkboard.

44. What do you call a book you write about yourself? *(Autobiography)*

45. What letters would form the call number for a book about Abraham Lincoln? *(Lin)*

46. Would a book about Abraham Lincoln be found at the beginning, middle, or end of the biography section? *(Middle)*

47. Would a book about John Henry be found in the biography section? *(No, folk heroes are classified under nonfiction)*

48. What page in a book lists the chapters? *(Contents)*

49. What part of a book has words in alphabetical order and gives page numbers for finding information? *(Index)*

50. Which is the best answer:

    The items on the contents page are arranged:

    a. alphabetically by stories
    b. alphabetically by authors' names
    c. sequentially by page numbers *(C)*

51. In our card catalog, what does a color band indicate? *(Nonbook)*

52. Name a nonbook material. *(Videotape, CD disk, audiotape, map)*

53. In what section of the library would you find short stories? *(Story collection)*

54. Where is our Story Collection?

55. What is the call number for story collection? *(SC)*

56. Is a book on Orville and Wilbur Wright a Story Collection or a Collective Biography? *(Collective Biography)*

57. Are stories about Encyclopedia Brown classified as a Story Collection? *(Yes)*

58. How often are the Caldecott and Newbery Medals awarded? *(Annually)*

59. For what reason is Caldecott given? *(Best illustrations)*

60. For what reason is Newbery given? *(Best children's story)*

61. Which award—the Newbery or the Caldecott—is pictured with a man on a horse? *(Caldecott)*

62. Give the title of a book that has won an award.

63. Which one of these fiction books would come first on the shelf—*The High King* by Lloyd Alexander; *Blubber* by Judy Blume? *(The High King)*

64. What is historical fiction? *(Fiction set in an historical period)*

65. Give an example of historical fiction.

66. Is a *Wrinkle in Time* historical fiction? *(No)*

67. Give an example of a nonfiction subject.

68. Where are our nonfiction books in the library?

69. Where are our biography books in the library.

70. Where are our intermediate fiction books in the library?

71. Where are our picture books or easy fiction books located in the library?

72. Where are our nonbook materials located?

73. What is an atlas? *(Book of maps)*

74. In what section are the atlases found? *(Reference)*

75. What is a set of books with information on people, places, things, and events called? *(Encyclopedia)*

76. What is each book in an encyclopedia set called? *(Volume)*

77. Which volume has an alphabetical listing with volume and page numbers of subjects covered in the encyclopedia? *(Index volume)*

78. Which dictionary has more word entries, the abridged or unabridged? *(Unabridged)*

79. What kind of dictionary is a dictionary of people? *(Biographical dictionary)*

80. Name three types of information found in a dictionary. *(Definitions; pronunciation; parts of speech; spelling)*

Sample Questions

81. What reference book has information on major events that took place during the previous year? *(Almanac)*

82. In our library, what is the call number for a filmstrip? *(FS)*

83. In our library, what is the call number for a filmstrip with a record? *(FS/S)*

84. In our library, what is the call number for a record? *(R)*

85. What are the three major parts to a computer? *(Monitor; keyboard; disk drive)*

86. Where are the pages of a book sewn together? *(Spine)*

87. What is a short dictionary at the end of a book called? *(Glossary)*

88. What is a list of books on a subject called? *(Bibliography)*

89. An introduction to the book is found in the _____. *(Foreword)*

90. Name a periodical we have in our library.

91. Why is the library called a media center? *(It has both book and nonbook material)*

92. Why is the librarian called a media specialist? *(The librarian is also in charge of audio-visual materials and equipment)*

93. Give three rules for proper care of books.

94. Give three rules to follow in the media center.

95. Give three rules to follow in the computer lab.

Game Finder Index